Annette Norma Weekes was born in Guyana and moved to England in 1961. She lives in south London with her two daughters, Esther and singer/composer Des'ree.

Vegetarian Cooking

CARIBBEAN STYLE

Annette Norma Weekes

ARP

Angela Royal Publishing

Published by ANGELA ROYAL PUBLISHING LTD
Suite 53, Eurolink Business Centre, 49 Effra Road, London SW2 1BZ

First published October 1996
1 3 5 7 9 10 8 6 4 2

A CIP catalogue for this book is available from the British Library
ISBN 1-899860-20-7

Design & typesetting by Nick Awde/Desert♥Hearts
Photographs by Gloria Nicol
Photographs pages 11, 14 & 18 by Annette Norma Weekes
Printed in Singapore by Imago

Contents

Author's Introduction

Food influences our lives in so many ways and eating healthily is vital to our very existence, especially in this day and age of fast food and food fads. I dedicate this book to my two daughters, Des'ree and Esther, who helped to change the way I eat.

When they announced that they were becoming vegetarians back in 1988, I thought it was just a phase and that it would not last, but it did and as the saying goes: "If you can't beat them, join them."

My imaginary playing at cooking when I was a young girl in Guyana was as real as you can get it, none of your pretend stuff. I would acually raid the food cupboard or 'safe', as we called it. During school holidays at playtime we would gather twigs, make a real fire in the yard and set about cooking in small pots and dolls' utensils. Yes, my few toys always included kitchen utensils and my 'mix-ups' were always tasty. As an adult I chose nursing as my career but, although it became my first love, cooking always was and still is my first passion.

Becoming a vegetarian has made me rethink my whole approach to food. 'Vegetarian Cooking Caribbean Style' is a challenge to recreate some traditional dishes as well as creating some exciting new ones based on Caribbean ingredients without using meat or fish, yet satisfying my well-developed taste buds and those of my children. I can truly say that I have never felt so good, so healthy and full of life. I even seem to be getting younger, according to my friends.

Yes, food is my passion. I love food – creating, eating and sharing it with my friends and family. I am so pleased to be able to share it with you too.

I am grateful to Tony Fairweather for having faith in me, and to Angela Royal & Gloria Nicol for making this project a pleasure from beginning to end.

Annette Norma Weekes

YOU ARE WHAT YOU EAT

Most of the ingredients, herbs and spices used in these recipes have their origins in Africa and the Caribbean. Some of you will find a few of these recipes familiar, others are new, exciting and different – feel free to add touches of your own.

All of these dishes are nutritional and very satisfying. They can can be made low fat or low calorie by using reduced fat/calorie options for milk, butter, sugar and so on.

Vegetarianism is a safe and healthy life-style. We only need to think a little harder when creating menus, but a little imagination and creativity, along with a few herbs and spices, can create simple and tasty dishes for all ocassions. There is no reason to feel malnourished. All the required nutrients can be obtained from vegetables, nuts, beans, pulses, and fruits.

Ever since I can remember, I have admired colourful fruits and vegetables and imagined how I would cook them to make them taste as stunning as they look. Yellow, red, orange, green, and even purple – there is no reason why our foods should not be colourful as the clothes and accessories we wear.

CATEGORIES OF FOOD
FOR HEALTHY EATING

VEGETABLES
ackee
aubergine
okra
marrow
christophine
butternut squash
cauliflower
broccoli
corilla
runner beans
bora long bean
cabbage
spinach
pumpkin
greens
callaloo
cucumber
carrot
chinese cab ball
pepper / capsicum

CARBOHYDRATES
sweet
potato
yam
plantain
eddoe
potato
breadfruit
tania
rice
green banana

PROTEIN
blackeye bean
kidney bean
aduki bean
soya bean
chick pea
split pea
pigeon pea
lentils
peanut
pine nut
coconut
cashew nut
brazil nut
pistachio nut

FRUIT
pineapple
banana
orange
melon
gooseberry
mango
pear
avocado
apple
grape
peach
passion fruit
soursop
water melon

HERBS AND SPICES

Below are a few examples of herbs and spices familiar to Caribbean cooking, some can be used medicinally.

Spices

Bayleaf – a well known leaf with a strong aroma when crushed. It is used in soups, stews, gravies, savoury rice dishes, marinades, porridges and in bouquet garni. It also flavours milk and condiments, if possible try to use fresh leaves.

Cinnamon – the bark, whole or ground, is a popular spice and is used in cakes and other baked foods. It is also used in sauces, sweets, pickles, vinegars and teas – a hot cup of cinnamon tea is very warming on a chilly evening.

Hot pepper – e.g. chillies, scotch bonnet, paprika. There are two main types of pepper – chilli peppers and sweet peppers. Chilli peppers are small red or green (and sometimes yellow) fruit – varying from mild to very hot – which are used to impart a hot spicy taste to soups, stews, and sauces. The vitamin content does not contribute greatly to the nutritional value due to the small amount used per dish.

Nutmeg – another very popular spice. A little nutmeg grated in puddings, fruit, alcoholic beverages and sauces adds a 'spiced' flavour.

Mace – the reddish net-like wrapping around the nutmeg's hard outer covering. When dried, mace changes to a yellow colour and can be used whole or ground. It is one of the strongest spices and should be used sparingly. It has a mild nutmeg-like flavour and is used to flavour soups and sauces. It is especially good in pumpkin dishes.

Cloves – a dried flower bud that can be used whole or ground. It is commonly used to season hams and in preserves and pickles. Cloves add a subtle flavour to alcoholic and non-alcoholic beverages. Clove oil is commonly used to combat tooth ache.

Pimentos – these small, hot, aromatic seeds are used whole or ground to flavour pickles, marinades, stews and soups.

Turmeric – dried and ground turmeric is used in curries and for colouring rice dishes, pickles and salad dressings – a true saffron substitute.

Ginger – one of the oldest known and most widely used of the spices. Ginger is used fresh, dried and ground in preserves, curries, puddings, cakes, in Chinese cooking, beverages and as a hot spicy tea for colds, indigestion and for lowering temperatures during a fever.

Aniseed – is familiar to most people as a flavouring in bread, but is also very useful for calming digestive problems, especially colic in babies.

Cumin – a very pungent, ancient spice used in curries and stews. It complements squash, marrows and is also good in chutneys.

Vanilla – this dried, cured fruit or bean is a native Mexican orchid. The flavour and scent is familiar due to its use in everything from cream soda to cakes and ice creams. Vanilla extract is widely available.

Herbs

Coriander – an ancient aromatic herb used in cooking as a basic flavouring for curries, chutneys, pickles and dips. It has a distinctive flavour and is also good for garnishing.

Thyme – this well known herb is used to flavour stuffings, soups, stews and many other dishes.

Parsley – the most popular garnish and flavouring for stews, stuffings, soups and sauces. When eaten after garlic it helps to freshen the breath.

Chives – tender green leaves with a mild onion flavour. Chives can be chopped into almost any kind of salad, cheese, or vegetable dish. Use to flavour or garnish.

Sage – used in many dishes, sauces and salads. Can be wholesome as a tea.

Garlic – a member of the onion family. Garlic enhances many dishes – Caribbean cooking is not the same without it – and is rich in vitamins.

HINTS FOR THE KITCHEN

Increasing & Decreasing

When increasing recipes, for example from 4 to 6 servings, increase each ingredient proportionally and increase the standard cooking time by 5 mins per extra pound of ingredients used. When decreasing recipes, decrease proportionally. For example from 4 to 2 servings – halve all ingredients, from 6 to 4 servings – decrease all ingredients by a third.

Useful Tips for 'Difficult' Ingredients

● When leaf vegetables are wilted or blemished, pick off and discard the brown leaves or edges and sprinkle with cool water. Wrap in a kitchen towel and refrigerate for an hour or two.

● To perk up lettuce, add lemon juice to a bowl of cold water and soak the lettuce for an hour or so.

● Hard as rock brown sugar will soften in a few hours if you

place a slice of bread in the jar and close the lid tightly.

● When measuring sticky liquids such as honey or syrup, first oil the measuring cup with cooking oil and then rinse it in warm water.

● When frying, turn a metal colander upside down over the pan or skillet. This allows steam to escape but keeps the fat from spattering.

● When beating egg whites, add a pinch of salt to make them fluff faster.

● When using wooden skewers, soak them in cold water before use – this helps stop them burning when grilling.

● Never boil coconut cream briskly – it may separate. It is better to use moderate heat and frequent stirring to aerate.

When Things Go Wrong . . .

● To colour gravy, put brown flour in the pan before adding water or stock – this also prevents lumpy gravy.

● To thicken gravy, try adding potato flakes or mashed potato instead of flour. Corn starch can also be used – mix a tablespoon of corn starch or corn flour into a paste with some cold water, gradually add it to the gravy stirring constantly until at the required thickness and bring to the boil.

● When soups or stews are too salty, add cut raw potatoes and discard them once they are cooked – they absorb the salt. Or you can simply add sugar or honey to taste.

When You're in a Hurry . . .

● Wrap avocados in a brown paper bag for a day or so to make them ripen more quickly.

- When trying to ripen fruits, remember that exposure to direct sunlight will make them soft not ripe.

- To ripen green bananas or green tomatoes more quickly, wrap them in a damp kitchen towel then place them in a paper bag.

- To bake potatoes in a hurry: peel and then boil them in salted water for 10 minutes or so before putting them to bake in a hot oven. Split potatoes lengthwise halfway through cooking.

- To chop onions without tears do any of the following:

    - Cut the root end of the onion last.

    - Refrigerate the onion before chopping.

    - Peel the onion under running water.

    - Peel and quarter the onion, then chop it in a food processor to the required texture (coarse or fine).

- To peel thin skinned fruit: place the fruit in a bowl, cover with boiling water, let it stand for 1 minute and then peel; or spear or fork the fruit, hold it over a flame until skin cracks and then peel it.

- For better meringues: add a teaspoon of cornflour or two drops of vinegar while whisking.

Microwave Ovens

- Many of the recipes included here can be cooked in a microwave oven – especially where vegetables are used – as the microwave mantains freshness and colour. Two points to remember are:

    - It is essential that you use the correct accessories indicated in your microwave oven manual.

    - Follow cooking instruction times for your particular oven carefully; reheating foods that have been in the fridge will take a little longer.

Pressure Cookers & Steamers

● The pressure cooker is a valuable kitchen utensil for vegetarian cooking especially where dried beans and peas (pulses) are used in recipes. Here are some cooking times for pulses if a pressure cooker is used:

- Aduki beans 5 mins
- Black eye beans 5 mins
- Chick peas (Channa) 20 mins
- Lentils 3 mins (no soaking)
- Mung beans 5 mins
- Soya beans 20 mins
- Red kidney beans 10 mins
- Gungo peas 15 mins
- Pigeon peas 20 mins
- Broad beans 15-20 mins
- Pinto beans 45 mins

As you can see, a pressure cooker can save you a lot of time.

● Most pulses should be soaked overnight, but this soaking time may be reduced to a minimum of an hour if you are using a pressure cooker. It is important to follow cooking instructions on the back of the packet as uncooked beans can be harmful.

● A steaming basket is another valuable utensil for the vegetarian kitchen. Steaming is great, not only does it allow the vegetables to retain most of their vitamins and minerals but also maintains their colour.

Using Tinned Foods

My recipes have been designed with fresh ingredients in mind.

This means that they tend to take a little longer to prepare. Canned foods, especially beans, can be substituted for convenience but may make a difference to the flavour and nutritional value of the dish.

Food Hygiene

● Wash hands thoroughly before preparing food and after going to the toilet.

● Keep pets away from food, dishes and worktops.

● Keep the kitchen clean, wash worktops and utensils between handling food which is to be cooked and food which is not.

● Prepare and store raw and uncooked food separate from cooked food e.g. if you eat meat or fish keep raw meat and raw fish at the bottom or below cooked food in the refrigerator so that it cannot drip into and spoil the cooked food.

● Chilled or frozen food should be placed in the refrigerator or freezer as soon as possible after purchase.

ESSENTIAL BASICS
FOR
CARIBBEAN
VEGETARIAN
COOKING

Vegetable Stock

Dry jerk seasoning

Coconut milk

VEGETABLE STOCK

This basic stock is a vital ingredient for soups and stews.
Vegetable stock cubes or vegetable boullion can
be substituted to save time.

MAKES 1 TO 1.5 LITRES OF STOCK
1 large onion, chopped
2 bay leaves
2 cloves garlic, chopped
2 carrots, diced
2 sticks celery, chopped
sprig of parsley
sprig of thyme
2 peppercorns, crushed
2 litres of water

● Put all the ingredients in a large saucepan and bring them to the boil. Simmer for about one hour. If you prefer a concentrated stock, simmer for a little longer until stock is well reduced in quantity. You may freeze the stock when it has cooled – or it will stay fresh in the fridge for two to three days.

DRY JERK SEASONING

These measurements will make 2 ounces of jerk seasoning
(2 tablespoons). For larger amounts, increase the
ingredients in proportion.

2 tsp ground dry thyme
1 tsp ground mixed spice
1 tsp dried chives
½ tsp sugar
½ tsp salt
½ tsp onion powder
½ tsp hot chilli powder (optional)
½ tsp garlic powder
¼ tsp nutmeg
¼ tsp ground cinnamon
¼ tsp coarsely ground pimentos
¼ tsp paprika

● Mix all the ingredients together and store them in a glass jar
in a cool, dry cupboard.

Coconut Milk

Coconut milk is used in quite a number of Caribbean dishes. The traditional way of making it may be time consuming but it is still the best.

MAKES 1 LITRE
2 whole dry coconuts
1 litre (35 fl oz) warm water

● Break the coconut into large pieces and remove the flesh carefully with a knife. Place half the coconut flesh and half the warm water together in a blender and blend for 5 minutes. Pour the blended coconut milk into a large jug.

● Blend the remaining coconut flesh and warm water together in the same way then pour into the jug. Cover and leave the coconut milk in the fridge to chill for half an hour.

● Once chilled, strain the coconut milk through a sieve into another jug, pressing out all the milk. Discard the husk. Alternatively, the husk can be returned to the blender with a little extra water to extract more flavour if necessary.

With this method the less water you use the thicker the milk will be.

SOUPS

These soups are filling, nutritious and delicious.
Adjust the size of your servings to make a starter,
a snack or a main meal.

Dumplings for soups

Yellow split peas soup

Okra and callaloo/spinach soup with

butter dumplings

Sweet potato and callaloo/watercress soup

Carrot and pumpkin soup

Green banana and coconut soup

DUMPLINGS FOR SOUP

These dumplings are wonderful in soups and casseroles.

60ml (2 fl oz) milk or water
100g (4 oz) flour
40g (1½ oz) margarine
25g (1 oz) sugar
1 tsp baking powder
½ tsp salt
pinch of nutmeg

● Sift the flour and baking powder into a bowl, rub in the margarine then add the salt, sugar and nutmeg. Stir in the milk or water to make a stiff dough, then knead the dough lightly with your fingers.

● Tear off golf ball sized pieces of dough and form them into round dumplings. Add them to the soup 8 to 10 minutes before the end of its cooking time. Do not overcook the dumplings or they will become hard and chewy.

YELLOW SPLIT PEAS SOUP

This soup reminds me of my childhood days when my grandmother would cook it slowly over a coal fire – to give it more flavour she said – and fill it with tiny dumplings and root vegetables. In our house we prefer to double up the quantity of split peas for a thick, creamy texture.

SERVES 4-6

250g (½ lb) yellow split peas	*sprig of fresh thyme*
½-1 litre (20-40 fl oz) vegetable stock	
1 tbsp vegetable gee or butter	
1 medium onion chopped	*salt and pepper to taste*
1 clove garlic finely chopped	*½ tsp curry powder*
¼ tsp cumin seeds parched and ground	
chopped fresh coriander for garnishing	

● Heat the gee or butter in a heavy duty saucepan, add the chopped onion and garlic and saute them for a few minutes. Next, add the hot water or vegetable stock and bring to the boil. Let it boil on a medium to high heat for 10 minutes, then lower the heat and simmer on a medium to low heat until the peas are almost cooked.

● Add the thyme, curry powder and cumin, then adjust to taste with salt and pepper. Continue to simmer, stirring occasionally until the texture is fairly smooth.

● If you prefer a creamy texture the soup can be cooled and put in food processor or blender for a minute or two. Re-heat before serving and garnish with chopped coriander.

OKRA AND CALLALOO/SPINACH SOUP WITH BUTTER DUMPLINGS

Callaloo is similar in taste to spinach and thrives in the Caribbean climate. There are a number of varieties all of which may be used in this recipe. It should be fairly easy to get tinned callaloo if fresh is not available. This soup is full of iron!

SERVES 4-6

250g (½ lb) okra or ladies fingers
500g (1 lb) callaloo or spinach   1 tbsp vegetable butter
1 onion, chopped   2 stalks celery, chopped
1 whole small hot pepper or hot chilli
2 litres (70 fl oz) vegetable stock or water

FOR THE BUTTER DUMPLINGS
50g (2 oz) plain flour   50g (2 oz) fine corn meal
3 oz milk   1 tsp sugar
pinch of salt

● Wash and slice the okras thinly, chop the onion and celery, then saute them together in the butter in a skillet or pot.

● Add the vegetable stock or water and the whole pepper, then simmer for 20 minutes, until the okras are cooked. Remove the whole pepper from the soup.

● Next, mix together all the ingredients for the dumplings to make a soft dough. Add the dumpling dough by the teaspoonful to the simmering soup. Add the chopped callaloo

26

or spinach to the soup and leave it to simmer in a medium to low heat for a further 10 minutes. By this time the dumplings will have cooked and will also have thickened the soup.

● Adjust the taste with salt if necessary and serve hot.

SWEET POTATO AND CALLALOO/WATERCRESS SOUP

This delicious soup can be served hot or cold.
Using callaloo rather than watercress gives it a true
Caribbean flavour.

SERVES 4-6

2 cups raw grated sweet potato
2 pints (40fl oz) vegetable stock/boullion
125ml (4 fl oz) single cream or soya cream
1 medium onion, chopped   ½ tsp mixed herbs
½ bunch of watercress or callaloo, finely chopped

● Peel and grate the sweet potato and boil it in the stock until cooked. Add the chopped onion and simmer for about 5 minutes. Remove the potato and onion bits from the stock and sieve them. Return the sieved potato and onion to the stock together with the chopped callaloo or watercress. Stir and adjust to taste.

● Garnish with a swirl of single cream or soya cream.

CARROT AND PUMPKIN SOUP

SERVES 4-6

450g (1lb) carrots, diced	*1 small hot pepper (if desired)*
450g (1lb) pumpkin, diced	*1 dessertspoon honey*
2 pints (40 fl oz) vegetable stock	*sprig of fresh thyme*
1 medium size onion, chopped	*1 tbsp vegetable gee or butter*
1 clove of garlic, chopped	*salt and pepper to taste*

chopped fresh coriander for garnishing

● Wash and dice the carrots. Peel, wash and remove the soft pith and seeds from pumpkin, then dice the pumpkin flesh. If you have an electric juicer, juice the carrots and pumpkin together, retaining both the juice and the residue. If a juice machine is not available, cook the pumpkin and carrots and sieve or process in a food processor. (Juicing is one way to preserve nutrients by avoiding overcooking.)

● Heat the gee or butter in a saucepan then saute the chopped the onion and garlic until they are translucent. Add the pumpkin and carrot residue and cook for a further 5 minutes.

● Add the vegetable stock to the saucepan along with honey, thyme, hot pepper and carrot and pumpkin juice. Bring the soup to the boil and let it simmer for 20 minutes. Remove the hot pepper.

● Season with salt and pepper to taste. Garnish with chopped coriander. If a smoother texture is preferred the soup may be liquidised or processed in a food processor before garnishing.

GREEN BANANA AND COCONUT SOUP

SERVES 4

4 green bananas
1 clove garlic, crushed
1 medium onion, chopped
225ml (8 fl oz) coconut milk
450ml (16 fl oz) vegetable stock
2 tbsp butter or vegetable oil

● Steam the green bananas in the skins until they are cooked (about 10 minutes). Remove their skins and puree them in a food processor for a few minutes.

● Fry the onion and garlic in the butter or vegetable oil until golden brown. Add the coconut milk and vegetable stock then simmer them gently for a few minutes. Add the pureed green bananas, salt and pepper and simmer the soup for a further 5 minutes.

● Garnish with sprig of thyme and serve with 'bakes' or 'floats' (see pages 137 and 145).

STARTERS, FINGER FOOD, SNACKS & SIDE DISHES

Mushrooms in white wine
Sweet potato chips
Savoury chick peas
Chick pea fritters
Herby black eye bean fritters
Cocktail cheese puffs
Stuffed baby tomatoes
Breadfruit croquettes
Phulourie
Mini stuffed dumpling surprises
Aubergine or egg plant choka
Potato nests with egg plant choka
Yam & spinach rissoles
Savoury pumpkin fritters
Carrot ramekins
Pumpkin pancakes
Peas and corn rice ring
Black eye peas & rice
Yellow & green split peas rice
Speedy potato pie

MUSHROOMS IN WHITE WINE

This starter is quick, easy and will leave your guests in raptures.

SERVES 3-4

225g (8 oz) button mushrooms   300ml (½ pt) dry white wine
1 garlic clove, crushed
1 medium onion, finely chopped
1 tbsp chopped fresh parsley   60ml (2 fl oz) fresh soured cream
salt to taste

● Put the mushrooms in a saucepan with the wine, garlic, onion and parsley. Bring them to the boil and leave them to simmer gently for 20 minutes. Remove the pan from the heat, stir in the soured cream and add salt to taste. Serve at once.

SWEET POTATO CHIPS

Chips can be made with a variety of ground vegetables
such as cassava, breadfruit, yams and even carrots.
They all have their own individual flavours.

SERVES 4-6

2 large sweet potatoes   1 tbsp lemon juice
1 tsp salt   sunflower cooking oil for frying

● Peel, wash and then slice the sweet potatoes into 3 inch long chunky chips. Let them stand in a bowl of water with lemon juice for 5 minutes – this will stop them discolouring.

● Steam or par boil the chips for 5 minutes then drain them.

● Shallow fry in sunflower oil until golden or brush with oil and bake in a moderately hot oven 180C (350F) or gas mark 4 for 15 minutes until golden. Serve hot either on their own or with a vegetarian burger.

VARIATION
You can spice up these chips by making
a simple marinade.

● Pour the marinade over the steamed or par boiled sweet potatoes, then bake them in the oven until crispy and golden brown.

● To make the marinade mix the following ingredients together:

1 tbsp soya sauce
1 tbsp honey
2 tbsp cooking oil
½ tsp dried herbs
½ tsp pepper sauce
2 tbsp sesame seeds

SAVOURY CHICK PEAS

I adore the versatility of chick peas – a robust pea with a very distinctive flavour and good for most vegetarian dishes. This dish is known as 'Channa' in my home island, Guyana. It is of Indian origin and is very nutritious, having a particularly high protein content. It makes a great snack or accompaniment to a main meal, as well as being a buffet favourite.

SERVES 4-6

175g (6 oz) chick peas   *½ red pepper*
2 medium size onions   *½ green pepper*
3 cloves garlic   *1 bay leaf*
1 medium size hot chilli (optional)
1-2 tsp savoury seasoning salt or vegetable bouillon
2 tbsp chopped parsley for garnishing (optional)
2 tbsp chopped spring onion   2 tbsp of vegetable or olive oil

● Soak the chick peas overnight. Drain off the soak water and cook the peas with the bay leaf until they are tender. Drain off the water and remove the bay leaf.

● Peel the onion and garlic and chop them coarsely. Wash and de-seed the pepper, wash the spring onion then chop them coursely in a food processor or by hand.

● Heat the oil to medium heat in a skillet or saucepan, add the chopped vegetables and saute them for three minutes. Add the chick peas, seasoning salt or bouillon and chopped chillies. Fry for a further 3 minutes stirring lightly with fork or wooden spoon until the chick peas and vegetables are well mixed together.

CHICK PEA FRITTERS

SERVES 6-8
175g (6 oz) chick peas
100g (4 oz) wholewheat flour
¼ tsp sea salt
1 large egg
1½ tsp baking powder
¼ pt water
2 tbsp vegetable cooking oil
1 bay leaf
½ tbsp chopped coriander
vegetable cooking oil for frying

● Soak the chick peas overnight, rinse them thoroughly, then boil them until tender. Drain off the water.

● Sieve the flour into a bowl together with the baking powder.

● Using a food processor or blender, process the chick peas to a batter-like consistency – if necessary do this in two batches. Add the flour and baking powder mixture, 2 tablespoons of cooking oil, egg, salt and water, then beat everything together to a soft batter.

● Heat enough cooking oil to deep fry, then drop in the batter one teaspoonful at a time and fry until golden. Drain on kitchen paper.

● Garnish with chopped coriander and serve warm if possible, with hot tomato sauce or a spicy dip.

HERBY BLACK EYE BEAN FRITTERS

I have always felt the eye of the bean to be symbolic,
however, in making this dish the skin and
the eye are removed.

SERVES 6
225g (8 oz) black eye beans
1 medium sized onion, chopped
2 cloves garlic
½ tsp pepper sauce or hot chopped chilli
2 tbsp finely chopped parsley
vegetable or corn oil for frying
white pepper and salt

● Soak the peas overnight in bowl of water. Make sure the water covers the peas. Drain the soak water away and add fresh water to cover the peas. Rub the peas with your hands to remove the skins – allow the peas to settle and the skins will float to the surface. Skim off the skins and drain away the water.

● Puree the peas, onion and garlic together in a food processor or blender. Pour the mixture into a bowl and add the hot pepper sauce, salt, chopped parsley, and white pepper. Adjust to taste.

● Heat the cooking oil in a deep saucepan and drop the batter into the hot oil a dessertspoonful at a time. Fry small batches at a time, turning regularly with a long handled slotted spoon until the fritters are cooked through and golden brown. Drain on kitchen paper.

COCKTAIL CHEESE PUFFS

These cheesy choux pastry puffs are great with pre-dinner drinks or as finger food at parties. They can be filled with various flavoured cheeses, such as mustard, chives, curry powder, chilli or any combination of your choice. These are always a great favourite with my guests.

SERVES 4-6

75g (3 oz) butter	*4 medium eggs, beaten*
½ tsp salt	*1 medium egg for glazing*
100g (4 oz) plain flour, sifted	*225 ml (8 fl oz) water*
pinch of white pepper	*pinch of grated nutmeg*
100g (4 oz) vegetarian cheese, grated	

● Pre-heat the oven to 200C (400F) or gas mark 6 then grease two baking sheets.

● Sift the flour into a heat-proof bowl. Bring the water to the boil in a medium sized saucepan then add the salt, butter and nutmeg and let it boil until the butter has melted. Remove the pan from the heat, and gradually add the hot liquid to the flour, beating it in with a wooden spoon or hand mixer until smooth.

● Pour the mixture into the saucepan and return it to the hob on a low heat. Beat the mixture swiftly for two minutes until it leaves the sides of the pan without sticking. Remove the saucepan from the heat and blend in the four beaten eggs a little at a time until the mixture is smooth. Beat the grated cheese into the choux mixture then spoon it into a piping bag.

41

● Using a large nozzle and holding the bag upright, pipe out teaspoonfuls of the mixture onto the greased baking sheets leaving five inch spaces between each puff. Brush the puffs with beaten egg to glaze and bake them in the pre-heated oven for 15 minutes, then reduce heat to 180C (350F) or gas mark 4 and cook for a further 10 minutes.

● Remove the puffs from the oven and make a very small slit in the top of each one to allow the steam to escape. Cool the puffs on wire racks.

STUFFED BABY TOMATOES

SERVES 8-10

16-20 baby tomatoes
175g (6 oz) vegetarian cheese, finely grated
1 tsp soft mustard
½ tsp ground white pepper
2 tbsp chopped chives

● Wash and cut the tops off the tomatoes and scoop out the seeds with a teaspoon or the smallest end of a melon-baller.

● Using a fork, mix the grated cheese, mustard, curry powder and white pepper together thoroughly in a bowl.

● Stuff the tomatoes with the cheese filling, garnish each one with chopped chives and arrange them on a platter.

BREADFRUIT CROQUETTES

The versatility of the breadfruit is known throughout
the Caribbean and because of its texture and taste, can be
cooked in several ways. The fruit originated from the South
Pacific and was first brought to the Caribbean by
Captain Bligh in 1793.

SERVES 4-6

½ medium size ripe (but not soft)breadfruit
1 egg, lightly beaten
100g (4 oz) vegetarian cheese, grated
½ tsp salt or coarse bouillon
175g (6 oz) golden breadcrumbs
vegetable oil for shallow frying
pepper to taste

● Peel, slice and steam the breadfruit until it is cooked, then
mash it whilst it is still warm. Add the grated cheese and
beaten egg, season with bouillon or salt. Shape the mixture into
sausage shapes and roll or dip them in the breadcrumbs.
Shallow fry the croquettes and leave them to drain on kitchen
paper. Serve hot as a starter or side dish.

PHULOURIE

SERVES 6-8

100g (4 oz) yellow split peas *2 tsp parsley, finely chopped*
1 medium onion, chopped *2 cloves garlic, chopped*
2 tbsp self raising flour *½ tsp cumin powder*
½ a red pepper, finely chopped
½ tsp hot pepper sauce or hot chopped chillies
½ tsp curry powder
salt and pepper to taste
water for batter
vegetable oil for frying

● Soak the split peas in water overnight or at least 1-2 hours before you are ready to prepare them. Drain off the surplus water and put the peas, chopped onion, garlic, hot pepper, cumin, curry powder and flour into a food processor or blender. Blend to a thick batter.

● Add the chopped red pepper to the batter and adjust the consistency of the batter if necessary using water. Season with salt and pepper to taste.

● Heat the oil until it is moderately hot then drop tablespoonfuls of the mixture into the hot oil to fry, turning ocassionally until cooked through and golden. Remove the phulourie from the oil and leave them to drain on kitchen paper towels. Fry in batches until all the mixture is used up. Garnish with chopped parsley and serve with chutney or hot spicy sauce.

MINI STUFFED DUMPLING SURPRISES

I call these dumplings 'surprises' because you never know what savoury delight you might bite into. You can also make sweet dumpling surprises by filling them with any fruit filling of your choice.

SERVES 4-6

DUMPLINGS

225g (8 oz) flour	*2 tsp baking powder*
1 tbsp margarine or butter	*½ cup milk or water*
½ tsp salt	*1 tsp sugar*

cooking oil for frying

SPINACH FILLING

225g (8oz) spinach, finely chopped
125g (4oz) spring onion, finely chopped

1 clove garlic, finely chopped	*1 tsp curry powder*

1 finely chopped hot chilli or 1 tsp pepper sauce
1 tsp vegetable gee or vegetable cooking oil
salt and pepper or vegetable bouillon to taste

● In a medium sized bowl, mix together all the ingredients for the dumplings, then knead the dough to a smooth texture. Cover the dough and set it aside.

● Saute the chopped garlic, spring onion, spinach and chillies in a little gee or oil for a few minutes – season to taste with salt, pepper and grated nutmeg, then set aside to cool.

● Meanwhile, on a floured surface, roll out the dough to half an inch thickness, then using a 2 inch pastry cutter, cut out as many

rounds as possible until all the dough is used up. Fill each round with ½ tsp of the spinach mixture, bring the edges together to seal and roll lightly in palms of your hands to form them into a ball.

● Deep fry the dumplings in medium-hot oil until they are cooked through and golden. Serve hot or cold.

AUBERGINE OR EGG PLANT CHOKA

I always remember my childhood days when we roasted egg plant and sweet potatoes on an open fire. Delicious!

SERVES 2-4
1 large whole aubergine
2 spring onions, finely chopped
1 large tomato, skinned and chopped
juice of 1 lemon
half a hot pepper or chilli, chopped
pinch of cumin powder   salt and black pepper

● Grill or roast the aubergine in the oven until the skin is shrivelled and soft. Allow it to cool. Scoop out the flesh, add the lemon juice and tomato, then mash with a fork. Add the spring onions, chilli, cumin, and salt and pepper to taste.

● Serve as a pate on crackers, toast or garlic bread for an hors d'oeuvre or snack. If you plan to serve the Aubergine Choka in the Potato Nests on the next page, you will need to double up all the ingredients to make twice the quantity of Choka.

POTATO NESTS
WITH AUBERGINE CHOKA

The recipe for the Aubergine Choka filling is on page 48.

SERVES 6-8

450g (1 lb) baking potatoes   *1 tbsp melted butter*
1 large onion, sliced   *½ tsp lemon juice*
2 tbsp vegetable oil   *½ tsp jerk seasoning*
vegetable boullion and salt to taste

● Peel and wash the potatoes. Place the whole potatoes in a saucepan with enough water to cover. Add the lemon juice and salt and leave them to simmer for about 5-10 minutes until they are barely cooked through. Drain the potatoes and leave them to cool down completely. When cooled, coarsely grate the potatoes, then season them with the jerk seasoning and vegetable boullion or salt.

● Pre-heat the oven to 220C (425F) or gas mark 7.

● Combine the oil and melted butter to grease 6-8 two inch deep mini muffin tins. Place two tablespoons of grated potatoes into each tin. Press down in the middle, shaping the sides to form a nest.

● Bake the nests for about 20 minutes or until golden brown, then turn them out of the muffin tins and stand them on paper towels. Spoon in the Aubergine Choka, garnish with fried onions and serve.

YAM AND SPINACH RISSOLES

You can make these rissoles large or small depending on
whether they are to be an accompaniment to
a main dish or an appetizer.

SERVES 4-6

1 kilo (2 lb) white yam
225g (8 oz) spinach
50g (2 oz) butter
1 medium size egg
125g (4 oz) breadcrumbs
½ tsp salt
¼ tsp pepper
vegetable oil for shallow frying

● Peel, wash and cut the yams, then steam or boil them until
they are cooked. Place the cooked yams in a large bowl and
mash them with the butter whilst they are still warm.

● Wash the spinach, then steam it for 2 minutes. Lightly beat
the egg and add it to the mashed yam together with the
steamed spinach.

● Season the rissole mixture with salt and pepper to taste, then
shape it into rounds and roll each one in breadcrumbs. Grill or
shallow fry until cooked through and golden brown.

Savoury Pumpkin Fritters

These pumpkin fritters can also be made sweet with
a pinch of cinnamon and honey or sugar.

SERVES 6-8

150g (5 oz) plain flour or organic flour
1 medium size egg, lightly beaten
225g (8 fl oz) water
225g (8 oz) pumpkin, grated
2 tsp baking powder
1½ tsp seasoning salt
1 pinch ground mace
vegetable oil for frying

● Sift the flour into a medium size bowl, add the beaten egg,
water, salt and pinch of ground mace and blend together until
the batter is smooth.

● Peel, wash and grate the pumpkin, then fold the grated
pumpkin into the batter. Chill the pumpkin batter in the fridge
for at least 10 minutes.

● Heat the oil in a frying pan and drop in a dessertspoonful of
batter at a time. Fry the fritters until they are cooked through
and golden brown. Drain on kitchen paper.

● Serve with a mustard or sweet pepper dip as a snack or
starter.

CARROT RAMEKINS

This is a very up-market way of serving carrots!

SERVES 4
2 large carrots, finely grated
1 egg yolk (medium size), beaten
1 egg white (medium size), lightly beaten
2 tbsp milk
1 tbsp onion, minced or finely chopped
½ tsp ground nutmeg
salt and pepper to taste
parsley for garnishing

● Pre-heat the oven to 180C (350F) or gas mark 4.

● Blend the grated carrots with the onion, nutmeg and milk. Season with salt and pepper to taste. Stir the egg yolk into the mixture, then fold in the egg white.

● Lightly grease 4 ramekin dishes and spoon the mixture equally into each. Bake in the oven for 30 minutes or until set. Garnish with parsley.

PUMPKIN PANCAKES

Pancakes have always been popular because
they are so versatile. These can be served traditionally
with lemon juice and sugar, or filled with a variety of
sweet or savoury fillings. They really are too good
to be eaten only on Shrove Tuesday.

SERVES 6-8

175g (6oz) plain flour
½ tsp salt
½ tsp baking powder
125 ml (4 fl oz) water
125 ml (4 fl oz) milk
100g (4oz) grated pumpkin
pinch of grated nutmeg or ground mace
cooking oil for frying

● Whisk together the flour, baking powder, salt water and milk
to make a pancake batter, then set the batter aside in the fridge
for 10 mins.

● Meanwhile, peel and grate the pumpkin coarsely and stir in
the ground mace or nutmeg. When the pancake batter is ready,
mix in the grated pumpkin.

● Fry each pancake in 1 dessertspoon of oil in a medium frying
pan.

PEAS AND CORN RICE RING

This colourful rice dish looks beautiful on a buffet table. Increase the quantity of ingredients if you are entertaining on a larger scale.

SERVES 4
100g (4 oz) white long grain rice
100g (4 oz) frozen corn niblets
100g (4 oz) frozen baby peas
pinch of ground tumeric or saffron
½ tsp salt

● Wash the rice, then cook it in boiling water with the salt and saffron/tumeric until it is tender (10-15 minutes). Drain and rinse well.

● Steam the corn niblets and baby peas for 3 minutes, then mix them together with the cooked rice.

● Pack the mixture tightly into a dampened 1½ pint ring mould (or larger if you have increased the ingredients). Set aside to cool for 20 minutes or until ready to serve.

● Before serving, invert the ring mould onto a large serving dish, tap lightly and remove the mould. You can fill the centre of the ring with any filling of your choice or simply with a bunch of celery.

● Serve cold.

BLACK EYE PEAS AND RICE

Peas and rice is a Caribbean must. Whatever beans you use, the combination is delicious served with stew. I double up the quantity of beans for more flavour.

SERVES 4-6

250g (12 oz) brown or white long grain rice
150g (6 oz) black eye peas

1 medium onion, chopped	*50 ml (2 fl oz) coconut cream*
250 ml (10fl oz) vegetable stock	*550 ml (20fl oz) boiling water*
1 bay leaf	*sprig of thyme*
1 tbsp chopped coriander	*1 green hot pepper (optional)*
3 tbsp vegetable gee or oil	*salt and pepper to taste*

● Cover the peas with cold water, leave them to soak overnight, then rinse them well. Saute the onion and peas together in a saucepan for 5 minutes, then add the washed rice and stir for a minute. Add the vegetable stock, boiling water and all the remaining ingredients except for the coconut cream. Cover and simmer for 10 minutes.

● Remove the bay leaf and the whole hot pepper, then add the coconut cream. Season with salt and pepper to taste. If all the liquid has dried out add a little more warm water to the rice. Continue to simmer until the rice is cooked (about 20-30 minutes), then fluff up with a fork. If you are using canned peas, drain the liquid from the can and add the peas to rice when it is almost cooked.

● Serve hot.

YELLOW AND GREEN SPLIT PEAS RICE

This is another colourful rice dish which always reminds me of the sunny, green Caribbean. It is so full of flavour it can be eaten alone with a simple gravy or as an accompaniment to a spicy vegetable stew or other main course dish.
I call this nutritional dish
'my high protein rice.'

SERVES 4-6

300g (12 oz) long grain rice	*2 cloves garlic, chopped*
salt and pepper to taste	*pinch of saffron*
100g (4 oz) yellow split peas	*1 vegetable stock cube*
100g (4oz) green split peas	*30 fl oz (1½ pints) vegetable stock*
½ a red pepper and ½ a green pepper, diced	
3 cardamom pods	*1 medium chopped onion*
fresh coriander leaves for garnish	
2 tbsp vegetable gee	*salt and pepper to taste*

● Saute the chopped onion and garlic in large saucepan for about 3 minutes. Add the rice, peppers and split peas and continue to saute for a few minutes more. Pour in the stock and add the cardamom pods, a pinch of saffron for colour, salt and pepper to taste. Cook on medium heat for 15-20 minutes.

● Remove the cardamom pods and stir the rice with a fork to evenly distribute the peas. The rice should be moist and fluffy.

● Butter 4-6 ramekin dishes or small bowls and fill them with the peas and rice. Turn the mouled rice out onto plates or a serving dish and garnish with coriander leaves.

● Serve hot.

SPEEDY SWEET POTATO PIE

This dish goes particularly well with Jerk Vegetables (page 67).

SERVES 4-6

75g (3 oz) butter or vegetable margarine
2-3 lbs sweet potatoes   5 pineapple slices
60ml (2½ fl oz) pineapple juice   5 whole or 10 half glacé cherries
1 tbsp lemon juice
2 tbsp milk   ½ tsp salt

● Peel the sweet potatoes, cut them into chunks and leave them to stand in a bowl of water with the lemon juice added for 5 to 10 minutes (the lemon juice prevents them becoming discoloured). Steam or boil the potatoes until they are cooked but not soft. Meanwhile preheat the oven to 200C (400F) or gas mark 6.

● When the potatoes are cooked, transfer them to a large bowl and mash them with the butter or margarine and the pineapple juice until fluffy. Transfer the creamed potatoes to a greased oven-proof dish, level the top, then garnish with the pineapple rings and one whole or two half glacé cherries in each ring. Bake on the top shelf of the oven for 10 minutes.

● Serve hot.

MAIN COURSES

Red kidney beans and oatmeal loaf with coconut sauce
Stuffed peppers with rice
Bean burgers with tomato chutney
Black eye bean lasagne
Jerk vegetables
Esther's mung bean shepherd's pie
Caribbean vegetable crumble
Omelettes stuffed with spinach
Christophine (cho cho) and butter nut squash cheese bake
Stewed okras
Metagee or 'oil down'
Okras au gratin
Mung bean curry
Curried vegetables
Ackee surprise
Ackee souffle
Stuffed courgettes
Red bean stew
Baked egg plant
Savoury stuffed pumpkin
Aubergine lasagne
Smoked tofu stir fry
'Ital' (spinach and okra)
Spinach and red pepper flan

RED KIDNEY BEANS AND OATMEAL LOAF WITH COCONUT SAUCE

This nutty, textured loaf is very economical and easy to make. Serve with the Coconut Sauce, and accompanied by fried plantain, tomato and cucumber salad.

VARIATIONS

1. Substitute soya mince, vegetarian stuffing or breadcrumbs instead of oatmeal
2. Substitute black eye beans for kidney beans to make a black eye bean loaf and serve with peanut sauce (see the recipe for Peanut Sauce on page 108).

SERVES 4-6

FOR THE LOAF	FOR THE COCONUT SAUCE
200g (8 oz) red beans	*1 large onion, chopped*
1 cup oats or oatmeal	*2 skinned tomatoes, chopped*
2 cloves garlic	*50g (2 oz) butter or*
1 medium onion,	*vegetable gee*
roughly chopped	*2 tsp soy sauce*
½ red pepper	*1 tsp brown sugar*
2 tsp vegetable boullion	*150 ml (5 fl oz) coconut milk*
2 tbsp chopped parsley	
2 tsp curry powder	
2 tbsp tomato purée	
salt and pepper to taste	
¼ cup roasted sunflower seeds	
1 bay leaf	

● Soak the beans overnight, then strain off the water and rinse them.

● Add the beans to a saucepan of fresh water, add a bay leaf, bring to the boil and cook slowly until the beans are tender (about 1 hour). Strain off the water and remove the bay leaf.

● Pre-heat the oven to 180C (350F) or gas mark 4.

● Meanwhile, place the chopped onion, garlic and red pepper in a food processor and chop finely. Alternatively, chop them finely by hand. Put the chopped vegetables in large bowl and set it aside.

● Blend the kidney beans in a food processor in two batches, then add the bean 'puree' and the sunflower seeds to the bowl with the chopped onion, red pepper and garlic.

● Oil a 2 pint loaf tin or deep oven-proof dish and spoon in the mixture. Pack firmly and leave it to stand for 5 minutes.

● Scatter a handful of sunflower seeds on top. Cover with foil or a dish lid and bake in the oven for 20 minutes. Allow the loaf to cool slightly before turning it out on plate.

TO MAKE UP THE COCONUT SAUCE

● Fry the onion in butter until caramelised. Add the curry powder and brown sugar. Next, add the chopped tomatoes, soya sauce and coconut milk. Cook gently for 5 minutes and serve hot with the loaf

STUFFED PEPPERS (CAPSICUMS) WITH RICE

Peppers are available in red, green, yellow or orange
and can be stuffed with white or brown rice or
stir-fried vegetables. If you do use brown rice
remember that it takes a little longer
than white rice to cook.

SERVES 4

125g (3oz) white or brown rice
4 sweet peppers
2 cloves garlic, chopped
1 medium onion, sliced
2 medium size tomatoes, chopped
300 ml (11 fl oz) water
2 tbsp vegetable oil or olive oil
1 sprig of thyme
1 tbsp parsley, finely chopped
seasoned salt and pepper to taste

● Heat 1 tablespoon of the oil in a medium sized saucepan. Add the washed rice, thyme, 1 tablespoon of sliced onion, seasoned salt and pepper and stir for a few minutes. Pour in the water, cover and simmer until the rice grains are tender.

● Slice off the stem end of the peppers (to about 1 inch deep) and put them to one side. Slice a slither off the bottom end of the peppers so they can stand upright. Remove the core and seeds from the peppers and discard. Fill the peppers with the seasoned rice, put their tops on and arrange them in a flameproof dish.

● Set the oven to pre-heat to 200C (400F) or gas mark 6.

● Meanwhile, chop the tomatoes and allow the juice to drain. Heat the remaining oil in a pan, add the chopped garlic and the remaining onion then fry gently for 5 minutes. Add the chopped tomatoes and salt to taste, then cover and leave to simmer for 10 minutes. Spoon the fried onion, tomato and garlic over the stuffed peppers and bake in the oven for 30 minutes.

● Serve hot or cold.

BEAN BURGERS (WITH TOMATO CHUTNEY)

These burgers are great served either alone or with burger buns or pitta bread and salad. The chutney gives them a zing.

SERVES 4-6

100g (4 oz) kidney beans, cooked
100g (4 oz) black eye beans, cooked
1 medium onion, finely chopped
2 cloves garlic, minced
1 tbsp tomato purée/sun-dried tomato purée
1 tsp of mixed herbs
a dash of angostura bitters
100g (4 oz) vegetarian stuffing/fresh breadcrumbs
salt and freshly ground black pepper

FOR THE CHUTNEY
2 tomatoes, chopped   2 tbsp tomato ketchup
½ tsp Tabasco or hot pepper sauce

● Using your hands, squeeze and blend all the beans together, then add the remaining ingredients and mix thoroughly. Season to taste and allow the mixture to stand for at least 20 minutes.

● Shape the bean mixture into burgers and shallow fry for 5-10 minutes, depending on the size of burgers, turning constantly. Serve hot.

● To make the chutney, simply mix all the ingredients together in a small bowl.

BLACK EYE BEAN LASAGNE

SERVES 4-6

450g (1 lb) black eye beans, cooked	*3 cloves garlic, finely chopped*
1 packet of lasagne	*50g (2 oz) vegetable gee*
2 large tomatoes, chopped	*100g (4 oz) vegetarian cheese*
1 large onion, chopped	*1 tsp jerk seasoning*

1 tsp brown sugar
1 vegetable stock cube or 2 tsp vegetable bouillon
1 tbsp vegetable and tomato purée
paprika to garnish

● Cook the lasagne sheets in rapidly boiling water following the instructions on the packet. Rinse in cold water to separate the sheets.

● In a medium size saucepan saute the onion and garlic in the gee until it is brownish in colour. Add the tomato purée and brown sugar, then stir. Dissolve the stockcube or bouillon in 10 fl oz of water, add it to the saucepan and simmer for 5 minutes. The sauce can be thickened up with 1 teaspoon of flour. Stir in the black eye beans with the jerk seasoning.

● Line a greased oven-proof dish with one sheet of lasagne. Spoon in a layer of bean sauce. Repeat this process until all the bean mixture is used up, finishing with a layer of lasagne. Sprinkle with cheese and dust the top with paprika. Cover the dish with foil and bake in a hot oven 220C (425F) or gas mark 7 for 20 minutes. Uncover and bake for a further 10 minutes until the top is golden brown.

JERK VEGETABLES

This is a filling and tasty vegetarian alternative to the traditional and much loved Jerk Pork or Chicken.

SERVES 4

1 red pepper
1 green pepper
1 yellow pepper
2 courgettes
1 large onion
1 large aubergine
4-6 cloves of garlic (optional)
2 corn on the cob
4 tbsp olive oil or vegetable oil
1½ tbsp Dry Jerk Seasoning (see page 21)

● Mix the dry jerk seasoning with 2 tablespoons of the oil in a small bowl and put it to one side. Slice the aubergine into a colander and sprinkle a teaspoon of salt over it. Leave it to drain for about 20 minutes.

● Meanwhile, de-seed the peppers and cut each one lengthwise into 6 pieces. Cut the courgettes into one inch slices. Peel the garlic and dice it. Cut the corn on the cob into one inch slices.

● Rinse the aubergines under cold water and pat them dry with absorbent kitchen paper. Put all the vegetables together in a large bowl and mix them together with the jerk paste. Cover and leave them to marinate in the fridge for at least half an hour.

● Pre-heat the oven to 190C (375F) or gas mark 5. Grease a shallow oven-proof dish with vegetable oil arrange the vegetables in the dish and sprinkle them with the remaining olive oil. Bake on the middle shelf of the oven for 20 to 30 minutes until cooked and slightly charred.

● Serve hot with rice and peas or sweet potato pie.

ESTHER'S MUNG BEAN SHEPHERD'S PIE

This recipe is named after my youngest daughter Esther because she created it. Ideally the mung beans should be soaked overnight. Alternatively a pressure cooker can speed up cooking.

SERVES 6
175g (6 oz) mung beans
500 ml (20 fl oz) boiling water
725g (1½ lb) potatoes
125 ml (4 fl oz) boiling water
100g (4 oz) sweetcorn
234g can pineapple pieces
50g (2oz) vegetarian cheese, grated
2 tbsp sun-dried tomato paste
100g (4oz) frozen peas
1 onion, chopped

2 tbsp vegetable bouillon
1 tbsp Tabasco or pepper sauce
2 cloves garlic, chopped or pressed
4 tbsp olive oil
2 tbsp honey
25g (1oz) butter
1 tbsp curry powder

● Cook the mung beans in 500 ml (20 fl oz) of rapidly boiling water for about 20 minutes – when cooked the beans should be soft but whole. Peel and chop the potatoes and put them on to boil ready for mashing.

● Meanwhile, fry the onion and garlic in 2 tablespoons of olive oil until golden brown then add the sweetcorn and fry gently for 5 minutes.

● Preheat the oven to 190C (375F) or gas mark 5.

● Mix together the honey, bouillon, tomato paste, hot pepper sauce and curry powder then add the mixture to 125 ml (4 fl oz) of boiling water to make a paste. Add the paste to the onion, garlic and corn to make a sauce and leave to simmer for a further 5 minutes. Add the sauce to the mung beans and mix them together well.

● Mash the potatoes adding butter or olive oil. Spoon the mung bean mixture into an oven proof dish and spread the mashed potato evenly over the top. Arrange the pineapple pieces on top of the mashed potato and sprinkle with the grated cheese. Bake in the oven until the topping is golden brown.

● Serve with a tossed salad.

CARIBBEAN VEGETABLE CRUMBLE

SERVES 4

1 large aubergine, chopped   *4 okras*
2 carrots, chopped   *2 cloves of garlic, finely chopped*
1 or 2 christophine (cho cho)   *75g (3oz) vegetable gee or butter*
2 medium sized tomatoes, chopped   *1 tbsp sesame seeds*
1 large onion, chopped   *1 tsp cajun seasoning*

FOR THE CRUMBLE TOPPING
50g (2 oz) dry vegetarian stuffing
50g (2 oz) wholemeal flout
75g (3 oz) butter

● Saute the onion and garlic in the vegetable gee or butter in a large saucepan for 5 minutes. Add all the remaining vegetables, apart from the tomatoes, stir and cook for a further 5 minutes. Add the tomatoes and cajun seasoning, stir and pour the vegetables into an oven-proof dish.

● Pre-heat the oven to 190C (375F) gas mark 5.

● Prepare the crumble topping by rubbing the butter into the vegetable stuffing and flour until it is crumbly. Sprinkle the crumble over the vegetables and garnish with sesame seeds.

● Bake in the oven for 20 minutes until the crumble is golden.

● Serve hot.

OMELETTE STUFFED WITH SPINACH

SERVES 2-4

275g (10oz) fresh spinach   *¼ tsp nutmeg, grated*
1 tsp sugar   *¼ tsp salt or vegetable boullion*
2 tsp soy sauce   *4 eggs*
vegetable cooking oil for frying

● Wash the spinach thoroughly, discard any tough stalks and steam for 3 minutes. Remove from heat and rinse with cold water. Drain out excess moisture.

● Sprinkle the spinach with the soy sauce, sugar and nutmeg, then form it into a roll. Divide the roll into two pieces and set them aside. Break the eggs into a bowl, add the vegetable boullion or salt and stir with a fork until they are thoroughly blended but not foaming.

● Gently heat an 8 inch frying pan and add just enough cooking oil to coat the surface of the pan. Pour half the egg mixture into the pan, tilt the pan quickly so the egg mixture coats the whole surface.

● When the egg is set and lightly brown on the underside, slide the omlette out onto grease-proof paper. Put one of the rolls of spinach rolls along the edge of the omelette and roll up the spinach in the omelette, squeeze lightly to firm up the roll. Pour the rest of egg mixture into the pan and repeat the process with the remaining egg and spinach.

● These omelette rolls may be eaten hot or left to cool and then cut into 1 inch slices for a buffet or light meal.

METAGEE OR 'OIL DOWN'

As a child, I enjoyed watching
my grandmother prepare all the ingredients for
the family's feast of Metagee – a time-consuming dish that
was well worth waiting for. In those days, coconut milk was
made from scratch, i.e. grating and 'washing' the grated
coconut in milk or water to obtain the coconut milk.
These days coconut milk is readily available tinned
or in powdered form. My recipe for making
traditional coconut milk is in the 'Essential
Basics' section (page 22).

SERVES 6-8
1 medium coconut
1 medium size cassava
1 medium size sweet potato
225g (8 oz) white yam
225g (8 oz) pumpkin or butternut squash
1 firm but not over-ripe plantain
2 medium green bananas
1 large onion, sliced
1 medium breadfruit, sliced (if available)
1 sprig thyme
600ml (20 fl oz) lukewarm water
one whole hot pepper (optional)
dumplings (optional)
salt and pepper

● Make up the coconut milk using 600ml lukewarm water. Peel
the vegetables, wash and cut them in large pieces, then arrange

them in a large saucepan. Top with the sliced onions, a sprig of thyme and the whole pepper. Sprinkle over a little salt and pepper. Add the coconut milk, cover and simmer until the vegetables are tender (about 20-30 minutes).

● Remove the hot pepper and add the dumplings for the last 8-10 minutes of cooking. Serve hot, garnished with chopped spring onions. Traditionally, Metagee is served on its own.

OKRA AU GRATIN

SERVES 4

12 small okras	*125g (4 oz) vegetarian cheese*
125g (4 oz) breadcrumbs	*2 tsp dry mustard*
50g (2 oz) butter or margarine	*2 tbsp water*

● Wash the okras, cut off their tips and stems and steam them in a saucepan until tender.

● Pre-heat the oven to 160C (325F) or gas mark 3.

● Grate the cheese. Make a basic white sauce, add the cheese and mustard. Adjust with salt to taste.

● Arrange the cooked okras in a greased oven-proof dish, sprinkle on the breadcrumbs and pour on the cheese sauce making sure everything is covered. Bake in the oven until lightly golden and bubbling.

MUNG BEAN CURRY

SERVES 4
225g (8 oz) mung beans
100g (4 oz) chopped tomatoes
225g (8 fl oz) vegetable stock
1 medium onion, chopped
2 cloves garlic, minced
1 tsp dried jerk seasoning
2 tbsp curry powder
¼ tsp ground cumin
2 tbsp vegetable oil
salt to taste

● Boil the mung beans in 30 fl oz of water for 20-30 minutes until tender. Drain but reserve the excess liquid if any – this may be used to make up your vegetable stock.

● In a heavy based saucepan fry the onion and garlic for one minute, add the mung beans and curry powder, and stir thoroughly. Add the chopped tomatoes, cumin and jerk seasoning and continue to stir for a further 2 minutes, then add the warm vegetable stock. Season to taste cover and simmer for 10-15 minutes.

● Serve with plain boiled rice or Paratha Roti. (See the recipe on page 144.)

CURRIED VEGETABLES

SERVES 4

225g (8oz) potatoes, cubed
225g (8oz) courgettes, sliced
1 medium size onion, chopped
100g (4oz) tomatoes, skinned and chopped
1 clove garlic, chopped
1 medium size aubergine, cut into chunks
2 tbsp curry powder or paste
1 tsp chopped coriander
2 tbsp vegetable gee
1 tbsp sesame oil
1 tbsp vegetable boullion
1 tsp pepper sauce or 1 tsp jerk seasoning
300ml (10 fl oz) hot water
2 tbsp coconut cream or coconut milk
salt

● Fry the onion and garlic in the vegetable gee in a large saucepan. Add the curry powder and stir. Add the potatoes and water, stir and leave to cook for 3 minutes.

● Add the aubergines and cook for a further 10 minutes or until the potatoes are almost cooked. Add the chopped tomatoes, courgettes, vegetable boullion and pepper sauce. Adjust to taste.

● Add the coconut cream or milk and simmer for 10-15 minutes. Serve in a large dish garnished with chopped coriander and accompanied by Paratha Roti or any rice dish of your choice.

ACKEE SURPRISE

SERVES 4
1 can of ackee
1 medium red onion, sliced
1 medium green pepper, sliced
1 medium red pepper, sliced
1 chilli pepper, sliced
salt to taste
1 clove garlic, crushed
1 tsp dry jerk seasoning
½ tsp paprika
chopped coriander leaves
3 tbsp sunflower oil

● Drain the ackees thoroughly and arrange them in shallow oven-proof dish. Reserve five or six for garnishing later on.

● Heat the oil in a frying pan, cook the onion and garlic gently for 3 minutes. Add the sliced peppers and continue to cook for a further 5 minutes. Add the jerk seasoning, sliced chillies and salt to taste.

● Spoon the cooked onion and pepper over the ackees in the oven-proof dish. Arrange the reserved ackees on top and dust with paprika.

● Bake in a moderately hot oven at 180C (375F) or gas mark 5 for 10 minutes. Garnish with chopped coriander and serve hot.

ACKEE SOUFFLÉ

This wonderfully light dish is a great alternative to
the traditional 'ackee and saltfish' and does not
sacrifice any of the quality and taste.

SERVES 4

3 tbsp butter	*4 egg yolks*
3 tbsp flour	*4 egg whites*
250 ml (10 fl oz) water	*1 tsp Worcester sauce*
250 ml (10 fl oz) milk	*½ tsp salt*
1 can of ackees	*¼ tsp white pepper*

● Drain the ackees thoroughly and set them aside.

● Melt the butter in a pan over moderate heat, then stir in the
flour. Add the milk and continue stirring until the mixture
thickens. Add the salt, pepper and Worcester sauce. Remove
the mixture from the heat and beat in the egg yolks one at a
time. Gently stir in the ackees, then leave the mixture to cool.

● Pre-heat the oven to 180C (375F) or gas mark 5. Butter the
casserole dish.

● Beat the egg whites until they are stiff enough to peak. Fold
them into the ackee mixture. Pour the soufflé mixture into a
buttered soufflé dish and bake in the oven for about 35 minutes
until the top is lightly brown.

STUFFED COURGETTES (ZUCCHINI)

SERVES 4
4 medium size courgettes
1 medium size onion, finely chopped
1 tsp mixed herbs
50g (2 oz) breadcrumbs
2 tbsp vegetable oil, sesame oil or olive oil
100g (4 oz) vegetarian cheese, grated
1 clove garlic, finely chopped
chopped parsley to garnish

● Wash the courgettes and cut them in half lengthways. Scoop out the flesh with a melon baller, if you have one, leaving a scalloped shell.

● To make the stuffing, saute the onion and garlic, then add the courgette flesh and the herbs. Cook for 4 minutes, remove from the heat and add the breadcrumbs, salt and pepper to taste.

● Pour a few drops of oil into the courgette shells, then fill them with stuffing. Top with grated cheese and grill until the cheese begins to melt.

● Garnish with chopped parsley before serving

Red Bean Stew

Red beans are very popular throughout the Caribbean and the method of cooking does not vary much from island to island. Red bean stew is delicious served with boiled rice, crusty bread or vegetables. Canned red beans can be used for this recipe to save time if desired.

SERVES 4

225g (8oz) red kidney beans
1 medium onion chopped
225g (8 oz) chopped tomatoes
2 cloves garlic, crushed
sprig of thyme
1 bay leaf
½ tsp freshly chopped chillies
1 tbsp sweet soy sauce
50ml (2fl oz) coconut cream or milk
175ml (6 fl oz) vegetable stock
2 dry cloves
2 tbsp vegetable gee

● Soak the beans overnight. Rinse them thoroughly and cook them until they are tender and the liquid almost gone.

● Saute the onion and garlic in gee or butter for a few minutes, then add all the ingredients except the coconut cream. Adjust to taste then leave to simmer for about 15 minutes. Add the coconut cream, then continue to simmer for a further 10 minutes.

BAKED EGG PLANT (AUBERGINE)

Baked egg plants are delicious. They are great when marinated before cooking and can be used as a sandwich filler too.
The tamarind in the sauce gives this dish a unique flavour.
If tamarind syrup is not available, mango chutney may be used.

SERVES 4

2 large aubergines	*2 tbsp vegetable oil*
1 onion, sliced	*2 tbsp of tomato purée*
2 cloves garlic	*salt and pepper*
1 red hot chilli pepper	*100ml (4fl oz) water*
2 tbsp tamarind syrup	

● Slice the aubergines into ½ inch thick rounds. Sprinkle them with salt and set them aside for 10-15 minutes.

● Pre-heat the oven to 200C (400F) or gas mark 6.

● Fry the garlic, onion and chilli together for 5 minutes. Mix the tamarind syrup and tomato purée together to make a sauce, then add the tamarind sauce and the water to the pan and simmer gently for 5-10 mins. Add salt and pepper to taste.

● Rinse and pat dry the aubergine slices, then arrange them on a flat greased baking dish or tray. Pour the sauce over the aubergines and bake uncovered in the oven for about 15 minutes.

● Serve hot with savoury rice or fresh bread.

SAVOURY STUFFED PUMPKIN

This visually stunning dish tastes every bit as good as it looks.

SERVES 4-6

1 medium size pumpkin
225g (8oz) soya mince, reconstituted
50g (2oz) green peas
1 tbsp ground cumin
⅓ tsp ground mace
2 medium sized onions, chopped
2 cloves garlic, chopped
½ tbsp sliced red pepper
½ tsp hot pepper or chillies (optional)
50ml (2 fl oz) vegetable gee or olive oil
1 tsp salt
1 tsp tomato purée

● Reconstitute the soya mince by soaking it in 250ml (10 fl oz) of warm water.

● Slice the top off the pumpkin and put it to one side. Scoop out the pumpkin's seeds and stringy fibres. Plunge the pumpkin into a large pan of boiling water add a half teaspoon of salt and boil until slightly tender to the point of a knife. Remove the pumpkin from the water carefully and drain it well.

● Pre-heat the oven to 180C (350F) or gas mark 5.

● Saute the onion and garlic, add the soya mince and cook for 5 minutes. Add the green peas, red pepper and hot pepper or

chillies if desired. Stir in the tomato purée, mace and salt to taste, then simmer for 3 minutes.

● Remove a thin slice from the bottom of the pumpkin to enable it to stand firmly on a dish. Spoon the filling into the pumpkin and cover with the pumpkin 'lid'.

● Place the stuffed pumpkin on a greased shallow dish and bake in the oven for 30 minutes. Leave the pumpkin to stand for 10-15 minutes before slicing into wedges.

● This very special dish presentation can be served hot or cold with crispy green salad or seasoned rice.

AUBERGINE OR EGG PLANT LASAGNE

This lasagne uses aubergine instead of pasta to make
a filling high protein meal.

SERVES 6
2-3 large aubergines
100g (4 oz) reconstituted soya mince
1 large onion, chopped
2 carrots, finely chopped
50g (2 oz) frozen petit pois
50g (2 oz) frozen sweetcorn
2 cloves garlic, finely chopped or pressed
50g (2 oz) vegetable gee or oil
100g (4 oz) vegetarian cheese, grated

Main Courses

2 tsp tomato purée
250mls (10 fl oz) vegetable stock
1 tsp mixed herbs
1 tsp sifted flour
2 tsp sesame seeds
salt and pepper to taste

● Preheat the oven to 190C (375F) or gas mark 5.

● Slice the aubergine into thick (5cm/2ins) slices and place them in a colander, sprinkle with salt and leave them to drain for 20 minutes.

● Saute the onion and garlic in a heavy based saucepan with vegetable gee or oil. Add the tomato purée and vegetable stock and simmer for 3-4 minutes. Add the reconstituted soya mince and continue to simmer. Add the mixed herbs, salt and pepper to taste, and flour to thicken. Finally add the corn and peas and simmer for a further 5 minutes.

● Rinse the aubergine slices under running cold water and pat dry with absorbent kitchen paper. Cover the bottom of a rectangular oven-proof dish with one layer of aubergine slices and pour a little of the soya mince sauce over them. Continue the layering process until the dish is full and all the aubergine and sauce used up.

● Cook in the middle of the oven for 15 to 20 minutes. Remove the dish from the oven, sprinkle with the grated cheese and sesame seeds then return to the oven for a further 5 to 10 minutes until the cheese has melted and turned golden brown. Serve hot with vegetables, baked potatoes or a salad of your choice.

SMOKED TOFU STIR FRY

SERVES 4

225g (8oz) smoked tofu
1 onion sliced
½ red pepper, sliced
½ tsp dry jerk seasoning
450g (1lb) broccoli florets
2 cloves garlic, crushed
3 tbsp sweet soy sauce
2 tbsp light soy sauce
3 tbsp vegetable oil
1 tbsp sesame oil
1 tbsp tomato purée
1 tbsp lime juice
1 tsp sliced green ginger

● Dice the smoked tofu into half inch pieces. Mix together the light and sweet soy sauces, lime juice and tomato purée, then leave the tofu to marinate in the mixture for at least 1 hour.

● Heat the oils together in a heavy duty saucepan or wok and saute the tofu for 5 minutes. Increase the heat and add the onions, pepper, broccoli, green ginger and jerk seasoning. Stir fry until the broccoli is just cooked but still crisp.

● Serve with boiled noodles or plain boiled rice.

'Ital' (Spinach and Okra)

This 'ital' rice is simply delicious and economical to prepare. The word 'ital' is a Rastafarian word and means the essence of things that are in their natural state. This dish is my adaptation of the original method.

SERVES 4-6

375g (13 oz) long grain or basmati rice
1 large onion, sliced   2 cloves garlic, chopped
225g (8 oz) fresh spinach   100g (4 oz) okras
1 red pepper, chopped   150 ml (6oz) coconut milk
450 ml (15 fl oz) vegetable stock
1 small whole chilli pepper
2 tbsp vegetable oil
salt and freshly ground black pepper

● Wash the rice well. Wash and drain spinach. Wash the okras, remove their tops and stems, then slice them.

● Heat a heavy based saucepan and fry the onion and garlic on a moderate heat for 3 minutes. Add the rice and continue to stir until both the rice and onion are translucent. Add the spinach, okras, red pepper and vegetable stock. Bring to the boil, cover and simmer until the rice grains are half cooked.

● Next, add the whole chilli pepper, season with salt and pepper to taste, pour on the coconut milk, stir lightly with a fork, cover and simmer on low heat until all liquid is absorbed into the rice. Remove the chilli pepper before serving.

SPINACH AND RED PEPPER FLAN

SERVES 4-6

225g (8 oz) spinach	*100g (4 oz) butter*
1 medium red pepper, sliced	*2 tbsp soya milk*
1 medium onion, sliced	*a pinch of grated nutmeg*
175g (6 oz) plain/wholemeal flour	*1 tbsp vegetable oil*
3 eggs plus 1 egg yolk	*sunflower seeds*
50g (2 oz) oats	*salt and pepper to taste*

● Put the flour and a teaspoon of salt into a bowl, then rub in the butter until the mixture resembles breadcrumbs. Add the beaten egg yolk and enough water to bind the mixture into a medium soft dough. Knead the dough gently on a floured surface. Roll out the dough to fit a 20cm (8 ins) flan dish or tin. Mould it into the tin, prick the base and crimp edges, then leave it to chill in the fridge. Meanwhile, remove the stalks from the spinach and blanch or steam it for 1-2 minutes. Drain well.

● Pre-heat the oven and a baking tray to 200C (400F) or gas mark 6.

● Lightly fry the onions and arrange the spinach and red pepper in the flan case. Beat the eggs and brush the edges of the pastry with a little of the beaten egg.

● Mix together the rest of the beaten eggs, milk, grated cheese, nutmeg and a pinch of salt and pepper to taste. Pour the mixture into the flan case over the spinach and pepper, then and sprinkle with sunflower seeds. Place the flan on a baking tray in the oven and cook for about 30 minutes.

● Delicious served hot or cold as a main course with mixed salad.

SALADS, DRESSINGS, DIPS AND SAVOURY SAUCES

These salads can be served as accompaniments to main
courses or as light meals with crusty rolls or
pitta bread and dressings.

Hot vegetable salad
Rainbow salad
Breadfruit salad with avocado dressing
Pawpaw salad
Avocado salad
Avocado with raspberry vinegar
Avocado with spinach salad
Vinaigrette dressing
Garlic dip
Avocado dip
Onion sauce
Parsley sauce
Walnut butter sauce
Peanut sauce

HOT VEGETABLE SALAD

SERVES 2-4
1 large ripe firm plantain
1 medium size sweet potato
1 christophine (cho cho)
1 wedge of pumpkin
1 large courgette
1 large onion
2 tbsp olive oil
2 tsp vegetable seasoning or bouillon powder
1 tbsp finely chopped parsley

● Peel and slice all the vegetables into chunky one inch pieces.

● Steam the sweet potato for three minutes then add the remaining vegetables and steam them all for a further 10 to 15 minutes. Do not overcook the vegetables.

● Place the steamed vegetables in a large bowl and toss with olive oil, vegetable seasoning and chopped parsley.

● Serve hot.

RAINBOW SALAD WITH SESAME DRESSING

SERVES 3-4

2 courgettes
2 carrots
1 red pepper
½ small baby nut squash
½ small hard white cabbage
a dozen green olives
chopped parsley

FOR THE DRESSING
1 tsp sea salt
1 tbsp lemon juice
3 tbsp olive oil
2 tbsp sesame oil
1 tbsp wine vinegar

● Wash and cut vegetables into thin strips, then steam them for 2 minutes or microwave steam (according to instructions) for 1 minute.

● Prepare dressing and spoon over vegetables. Garnish with chopped parsley and olives.

● Serve hot or cold.

BREADFRUIT SALAD
WITH AVOCADO DRESSING

SERVES 4-6

2 medium avocados
1 small breadfruit
125 ml (4 fl oz) sour cream
65 ml (2½ fl oz) mayonnaise
65 ml (2½ fl oz) virgin olive oil
2 tbsp fresh lime juice
1 tbsp finely chopped onion
1 tsp coriander leaves
¼ tsp chopped chillies
salt and pepper to taste

● Peel the breadfruit, cut it in quarter remove the heart and discard it. Boil the breadfruit until cooked but firm, then leave it to cool.

● Meanwhile, peel and half the avocados, discard the seeds and put the avocado flesh in a food processor with the lime juice, onion, coriander and chillies. Blend the vegetables to a purée. Gradually add the olive oil and season to taste with salt and pepper.

● Pour the mixture into a bowl and whisk in the sour cream and mayonnaise.

● Cut the breadfruit into bite-size pieces and pour the dressing over. Cover and refrigerate until ready to serve.

Pawpaw (Papaya) Salad with Lime Dressing

Pawpaw with its vibrant yellow or orange coloured flesh (when ripe) is a very popular tropical fruit and is available in most supermarkets. Pawpaw is sometimes used green in curries.

SERVES 3-4

1 large pawpaw (papaya)
6 tsp lime juice
1 tbsp brown sugar
2 tsp chilli sauce
1 tsp runny honey (optional)
1 small flat-leaf lettuce
2 spring onions

● Wash the pawpaw, cut it in half and remove the seeds and stringy membrane. Peel the pawpaw, then cut it into medium size cubes and put them in bowl.

● For the dressing, mix together the lime juice and sugar. Add chilli sauce and honey if desired, then set aside.

● Meanwhile, slice the spring onions lengthwise thinly then snip them in half. Wash the lettuce leaves and dry out the excess water. Arrange the lettuce leaves on a platter and pile the pawpaw cubes on top.

● Pour over the lime dressing and garnish with spring onion.

Avocado Salad

SERVES 4
2 or 3 medium size avocados
2 tbsp chives or green onions, finely chopped
2 tbsp parsley, finely chopped
2 tbsp lemon juice
1 clove garlic, crushed or pressed
65 ml (2½ fl oz) olive oil
1 tbsp sesame oil
2 tsp wine vinegar
½ tsp freshly ground black pepper
1 tsp sea salt
1 tsp sugar optional

● To make the dressing, mix the salt, pepper and sugar, add the vinegar and oils, then stir well. Finally, add the garlic, chives and parsley.

● For the salad, peel and slice them. Arrange the slices on a platter, dribble the lemon juice over them, then pour on the dressing.

● Serve as soon as possible – avocados discolour very quickly.

AVOCADO WITH RASPBERRY VINEGAR

SERVES 4

125g (4 oz) fresh or frozen raspberries
75 ml (3 fl oz) white wine vinegar
45 ml (2 fl oz) olive oil
75 ml (3 fl oz) polyunsaturated oil
2 firm ripe avocados
1 small radicchio lettuce

● Place half the raspberries in a bowl. Heat the vinegar until it begins to bubble, then pour it over the raspberries and leave them to steep for 50 minutes.

● Strain the rasperries, pressing the fruit gently to extract all the juices but not the pulp. Whisk the strained raspberry vinegar together with the oils and seasoning. Set it aside.

● Carefully half each avocado and twist out the stone. Peel away the skin and slice the flesh straight into the dressing. Stir gently until the avocados are completely covered in the dressing. Cover tightly and chill it in the fridge for about 2 hours.

● Meanwhile, separate the radicchio leaves, rinse and drain them, then dry them on kitchen paper. Store them in the fridge in a polythene bag.

● To serve, place a few radicchio leaves on individual plates. Spoon on the avocado mixture and garnish with the remaining raspberries.

AVOCADO WITH SPINACH SALAD

SERVES 3-4

1 large avocado
225g (8 oz) baby spinach leaves
2 onions, sliced thinly
2 tbsp olive oil
1 tbsp sesame oil
75 ml (3 fl oz) mayonnaise or salad cream
1 tbsp lemon juice
1 clove garlic, minced or pressed
4-6 leaves cos lettuce
boiling water

● Wash the spinach leaves and put them in a bowl, pour boiling water over them, leave them for 2-3 minutes and then drain.

● Heat the oils together and saute the onion and garlic until translucent but not brown.

● Peel and halve the avocados, discard the seeds, then dice the avocados and add lemon juice to help keep the colour.

● Put the spinach in a bowl with the sauted onion and garlic. Add the mayonnaise or salad dressing and diced avocado. Mix together lightly with a fork and serve on a bed of lettuce leaves.

VINAIGRETTE DRESSING

125 ml (4 fl oz) olive oil
2 tbsp wine vinegar
2 cloves garlic, pressed or juiced
¼ tsp dry mustard
¼ tsp Tabasco or pepper sauce
1 tbsp lemon juice.
glass jar with airtight screw top

● Place all the ingredients in the jar and shake vigorously until they emulsify, then store in the glass jar in the fridge. The dressing will stay fresh for about 1 week.

GARLIC DIP

2 garlic cloves, crushed
90 ml (3½ fl oz) yoghurt
90 ml (3½ fl oz) mayonnaise
¼ tsp Tabasco or hot pepper sauce

● Combine all the ingredients and stir well. Store in the fridge in a covered bowl or jar until ready to serve.

Avocado Dip

This dip is delicious served with crudites of raw vegetables
such as carrots, celery, courgettes and florets
of cauliflower or broccoli.

1 large firm ripe avocado
50 g (2oz) low fat cottage cheese
1 tsp lime or lemon juice
1 tsp minced parsley
salt and freshly ground black pepper

● Cut the avocado in half and discard the seed. Scoop out the flesh leaving the shell intact. Blend or mash the flesh together with the lime or lemon juice and the cottage cheese. Fold in the minced parsley and season with salt and pepper to taste. Pile into the reserved halved shells or the dish of your choice to scrve.

ONION SAUCE

This sauce can be used instead of gravy with
hot vegetables or a main meal.

SERVES 4

450g (1 lb) onion, thinly sliced
600 ml (20 fl oz) milk
150 ml (5 fl oz) single cream
1 tbsp wet mustard
½ tsp white pepper
½ tsp salt

● Put the sliced onions and milk into a medium sized saucepan
and cook gently until the onions are tender. Strain off the
liquid and rub the onion through a sieve. Return the milk to a
very low heat and simmer until it reduces to about half the
quantity. Stir in the onion purée and mustard. Adjust to taste
with salt and pepper.

PARSLEY SAUCE

This sauce is particularly good poured over hot baked potatoes.

SERVES 4

25g (1 oz) butter	*50g (2 oz) flour*
125 ml (4 fl oz) single cream	*125 ml (4 fl oz) milk*
1 egg yolk	*2 tbsp fresh parsley, chopped*
1 tsp dry mustard	*salt and pepper*

● Melt the butter in a saucepan. Stir in the flour and mustard, then slowly add cream and milk. Bring to the boil, stirring until thickened. Whisk the egg yolk, add it to saucepan and mix everything together. Season to taste with salt and pepper. Sprinkle with chopped parsley.

WALNUT BUTTER SAUCE

A delicious variation to the butter sauce which can be poured over hot vegetables.

SERVES 4

2 tbsp ground walnuts	*100g (4 oz) butter*
1 tsp wet mustard	*125 ml (4 fl oz) vegetable stock*
salt and pepper	

● Melt the butter in a saucepan and add the ground walnuts. Stir for a few minutes taking care not to let it burn. Add the stock, salt and pepper to taste and simmer slowly for 5 minutes. Serve hot.

PEANUT SAUCE

This goes well with the Black Eye Bean Loaf (see page 60) or Jerk Vegetables (see page 67).

SERVES 4

3 tbsp crunchy peanut butter
125 ml (4 fl oz) coconut cream
1 tbsp brown sugar
½ tsp grated ginger
½ tsp basil, finely chopped
½ tsp seeded red chillies
125 ml (4 fl oz) vegetable oil
1 tsp garlic, finely chopped

● Saute the garlic in the oil, for a minute or so. Add the chilli and ginger and continue to cook for 1 minute. Add the remaining ingredients except the basil and stir. Continue to simmer slowly until the sauce thickens.

● Pour into a shallow dish and garnish with chopped basil.

DESSERTS, CAKES, BREADS, PASTRIES AND SWEET SAUCES

Rum butter
Brandy butter
Banana & strawberry
yoghurt
Soursop ice cream
Almond ice cream
Vanilla ice cream
Pineapple sherbet
Tropical fruit salad
Tropical fruit trifle
Mango & coconut puff
pastry pie
Coffee meringue pyramids
Tropical fruit crumble
Avocado cream
Baked apple & coconut
pudding

Baked mango & bananas
Coconut ice
Cassava pone
Auntie's coconut bread
Coconut buns
Coconut & raisin loaf or
plait
'Cut & come again' cake
Rich orange sponge cake
Crusty bread rolls
Cottage loaf
Bakes
Savoury bread plait
Pancakes
Mung bean patties
Paratha roti
Floats

RUM BUTTER

This rich sauce is a delicious topping for fruit pies
or crumbles and sweet pastries.

SERVES 4

100g (4 oz) unsalted butter   100g (4 oz) soft brown sugar
90 ml (3½ fl oz) light brown rum
pinch of grated nutmeg

● Beat the butter and sugar together gradually until they are
creamy. Add a pinch of nutmeg and the rum. Continue to beat
for a further 3 minutes. Transfer to a jar, cover and leave in the
fridge to chill.

BRANDY BUTTER

This can be used in a similar way to rum butter.

SERVES 6-8

225g (8 oz) unsalted butter   225g (8 oz) caster sugar
90 ml (3½ fl oz) brandy

● Cream the butter in a bowl. Gradually beat in the sugar and continue to beat until the butter is smooth and white. Beat in the brandy a little at a time. Cover and store in the fridge or a cool place.

BANANA AND STRAWBERRY YOGHURT

SERVES 4
4 ripe bananas
300g (12 oz) strawberries
275 ml (10 fl oz) natural yoghurt
1 tbsp lemon juice

● Peel the bananas, cut them up and mash them with the lemon juice. Add the yoghurt and mix well.

● Wash the strawberries and remove their leaves. Divide the strawberries between 4 balloon shaped glasses and top with the banana yoghurt.

● Chill in the fridge before serving.

SOURSOP ICE CREAM

Soursop ice cream is an all-time favourite of mine.
I remember as a child taking turns to churn the ice cream
maker with great expectations of the treat to come!

SERVES 6

1 ripe soursop
1 x 400g can of evaporated milk or soya cream
100g (4 oz) caster sugar
1 egg white, beaten

● Empty can or carton of milk into a fairly large bowl and leave it to chill in coldest part of the fridge for about 2 hours.

● Meanwhile, remove the skin from the soursop and rub the pulp through a sieve to extract the juice. Set the creamy soursop juice to one side.

● Next, whip the cold milk until it is thick and double its quantity. Add sugar slowly and continue whipping, add the soursop juice and fold in the beaten egg white. Quickly pour the mixture into a chilled plastic container. Cover and freeze for 2 hours until mushy.

● Remove the almost frozen ice cream from the freezer and beat well again. Return it to freezer to freeze until firm. Transfer the icecream to the fridge to soften slightly before serving.

ALMOND ICE CREAM

SERVES 6-8

50g (2 oz) blanched almonds
2 x 400g cans of evaporated milk or soya cream
100g (4 oz) caster sugar
1 tsp almond essence

● Blend 2 tablespoons of evaporated milk or soya cream together with the almonds in a blender. Pour the blended almonds into a bowl, add the remaining milk together with the sugar and almond essence. Whisk thoroughly.

● Pour the mixture into an ice cream mould or suitable freezing container and place in the freezer for 3-4 hours.

VANILLA ICE-CREAM

This wonderfully rich and decadent ice-cream will keep
for up to 1 week.

SERVES 4-6
*300 ml (11 fl oz) milk
1 vanilla pod or 3 tsp vanilla essence
1 egg
2 egg yolks
100g (4 oz) caster sugar
250 ml (10 fl oz) double cream*

● Heat the milk together with the vanilla essence or pod
bringing it almost to the boil. Leave it to infuse for 10-15
minutes, then remove the vanilla pod.

● Whisk the whole egg, egg yolks and sugar together until they
are pale. Stir in the vanilla milk and strain the mixture into a
clean pan. Heat the mixture slowly over a gentle heat, stirring
continuously until it thickens like custard. Pour the mixture
into a bowl and leave it to cool.

● Whip the cream lightly and fold it into the cold 'custard'.
Pour the mixture into a suitable freezing container, cover and
place in the freezer for about 1 hour. Remove the ice-cream
from the freezer and whisk it thoroughly. Return it to the
freezer and leave until completely frozen. Transfer it to the
fridge about half an hour before serving.

PINEAPPLE SHERBET

SERVES 4

1 sachet vegetable gelatin
2 tbsp cold water
225 ml (8 fl oz) evaporated milk
225g (8 oz) sugar
225g (8 oz) crushed pineapple
1 tsp vanilla essence
1 egg white, beaten

● Soften the gelatin in cold water in a cup and stand it over hot water to dissolve. Pour the gelatin into a bowl together with the milk, sugar, crushed pineapple and vanilla essence. Whip everything together for a few seconds.

● Pour the mixture into a suitable container and freeze for 1 hour. Remove the sherbet from the freezer and whip until smooth. Beat the egg white until it is frothy, then fold it into the sherbet. Return the sherbet to the freezer to freeze until firm.

TROPICAL FRUIT SALAD

This delicious summer dessert is very easy to prepare.

Hint: when a mango is ripe it has a sweet aroma, it should be firm yet yield to pressure. If it feels soft or mushy it is over ripe.

SERVES 6

1 large firm ripe mango
1 large banana
1 grapefruit
2 kiwi fruit
1 star fruit (carambola)
½ fresh pineapple or 1 tin pineapple in juice
juice of one lime
juice of one orange (preferably Jamaican)
1 tbsp honey
½ tsp mixed spice
½ tsp vanilla essence

● Peel and dice the mango, banana, pineapple and kiwi fruit. Slice the carambola and segment the grapefruit. Place all the fruits in a large bowl.

● Mix the lime juice, orange juice, honey, vanilla essence and mixed spice together, then pour it over the fruit and stir until all the fruit is covered with the mixture.

● Serve alone or with your favourite ice cream.

Tropical Fruit Trifle

Trifles have always been regarded as a special desert and are ideal for special occasions, especially since they can be made well in advance. This trifle may be decorated with whipped cream if liked.

SERVES 4-6

1 jam Swiss roll or sponge cake   600 ml (20 fl oz) warm custard
225g (8 oz) can sliced pineapple or pineapple chunks in juice
2 firm ripe bananas sliced
100 ml (10 fl oz) double cream or whipping cream
60 ml (2 fl oz) sweet sherry or light brown rum
2 tbsp chopped mixed nuts

● Slice the Swiss roll or sponge cake into 1 inch pieces and arrange them in a glass dish. Peel and slice the bananas and arrange the fruit around and in between the sponge cake.

● Drain the pineapple, reserving the juice. Mix 5 tablespoons of the pineapple juice with the sherry or rum, pour the mixture over the sponge and banana, then leave to stand for about 1 hour.

● After 1 hour, arrange the pineapple pieces on top of the sponge and banana – save some of the pineapple for garnishing later. Pour the warm custard over everything, cover the dish and leave it to cool. When cooled, scatter chopped nuts over the custard (or over the whipped cream topping if this has been added), dot with pieces of pineapple.

● Cover with cling film and return to the fridge until ready to serve.

MANGO AND COCONUT PUFF PASTRY PIE

This pie tastes great and looks wonderful
when cut into wedges to show its
white and orange layers.

SERVES 6-8

flesh of 1 coconut grated
2 firm ripe mangoes (or two tins of mangoes, well drained,
if mangoes are out of season)
450g (1 lb) puff pastry
1 egg
50g (2 oz) 4 tbsp caster sugar
1 tsp almond essence
¼ tsp grated nutmeg

● Break the coconut into large pieces and remove the flesh carefully with a knife. Grate the flesh on a hand grater or blend to a medium coarse constistency in a blender or food processor a little at a time at high speed. Put the grated coconut in a bowl, add the almond essence, 2 tablespoons of caster sugar, and grated nutmeg. Mix well and set to one side.

● Peel the mangoes, slice them into small pieces. Put them in a bowl, sprinkle with 2 tablespoons of sugar and set to one side.

● Preheat the oven to 200C (400F) or gas mark 6.

● Meanwhile, roll out the puff pastry to half an inch thickness

and line an 8 inch x 2 inch flan dish with it. Leave enough to make the top of the pie.

● Spread a layer of half the coconut in the lined flan dish, follow with a layer of half the mango, then another layer of the remainder of the coconut finishing off with a final layer of the remaining mango.

● Roll out the rest of the pastry to make the top of the pie. Pattern with a knife, brush with honey and bake in the oven for 30 to 35 minutes. Serve hot or cold on its own or with cream.

COFFEE MERINGUE PYRAMIDS

SERVES 4
4 egg whites
225g (8 oz) caster sugar
30g (1 oz) instant coffee
250 ml (10 fl oz) whipping cream
100g (4 oz) green grapes (preferably de-seeded)
100g (4 oz) black grapes (preferably de-seeded)
100g (4 oz) flaked almonds

● Cover two or three large baking sheets with grease-proof paper and draw circles of one inch in diameter.

● Put a large star nozzle in a piping bag, stand it in an upright jug and turn back the top of bag ready for filling.

● Pre-heat the oven to 100C (200F) or gas mark ¼.

● Put the egg whites and half the amount of caster sugar into a clean bowl over a saucepan of simmering water, making sure the bowl does not touch the water. Whisk until firm.

● Add the remaining sugar and the instant coffee a little at a time, beating after each addition.

● When the meringue mixture has 'peaked', spoon it into the piping bag and pipe it onto the prepared baking sheets in peak shapes to cover the 1 inch circles. Bake in the oven for 1½ hours until crisp and dry.

● Meanwhile, prepare the grapes by de-seeding (if necessary) and cutting in half. Whip the cream until it is stiff.

● To make up the pyramid, put a number of merigues closely together on a large serving plate to form a bottom layer, cover this layer with some of the cream, grapes and almonds. Repeat this process, slightly reducing the diameter of each layer, to form a pyramid. Decorate the top with flaked almonds, cream and grapes.

TROPICAL FRUIT CRUMBLE

SERVES 6

3 ripe firm mangoes, cubed
400g (14 oz) pineapple cubes or pieces
75g (3 oz) soft brown sugar
25g (1 oz) caster sugar
50g (2 oz) ground mixed nuts
175g (6 oz) wholewheat flour
75g (3 oz) butter
1 tbsp lime juice
½ tsp ground cinnamon

● Pre-heat the oven to 190C (375F) or gas mark 5.

● Put the mangoes and pineapple cubes into a bowl. Add the brown sugar, lemon juice and ground cinnamon. Mix lightly and set aside in a shallow oven-proof dish.

● Put the flour and butter into a bowl. Rub them together using your fingers until the butter is evenly distributed and the flour looks crumbly. Add the sugar and nuts and mix well. Spoon the crumble over the fruits.

● Bake in the oven for 30-40 minutes until the top is light brown. Remove from oven, cool slightly and dust with caster sugar. Serve with rum butter (see recipe on page 110) or single cream.

AVOCADO CREAM

This is the most simple and most delicious dessert.

SERVES 4-6
3 medium sized ripe avocados
1 x 400g can sweet condensed milk
1 tbsp lime or lemon juice
¼ tsp grated nutmeg
sprig of fresh mint leaves

● Peel the avocados, cut them roughly and place them in a blender together with the condensed milk, grated nutmeg and lime or lemon juice. Blend everything together until smooth and creamy. Pour into a medium sized bowl or individual serving bowls. Chill, garnish with mint and serve.

BAKED APPLE
AND COCONUT PUDDING

SERVES 6

finely grated rind and juice of 1 lemon
150g (5 oz) soft light brown sugar
6 medium eating apples
100g (4 oz) butter
2 eggs, separated
100g (4 oz) plain wholemeal flour
1½ tsp baking powder
25g (1 oz) desiccated coconut
4 tbsp apricot jam, warmed
toasted shredded coconut to decorate

● Pre-heat the oven to 170C (325F) or gas mark 3.

● Peel, core and slice the apples. Pour the lemon juice into a large bowl, stir in 2 tablespoons of sugar and add the apples, making sure they are well coated.

● Gradually beat 4 oz of sugar into the butter until well blended. Add the lemon rind, then beat in the egg yolks one at a time. Stir in the flour, baking powder and desiccated coconut.

● Whisk the egg whites until they are stiff but not dry, then fold them into the creamed ingredients. Spoon them into a lightly greased 20-25.5cm (8-10 inch) fluted flan dish. Press the apples into the mixture, spooning the juice over them.

● Stand the dish on a baking tray or sheet and bake in the oven for for 1 to 1 ¼ hours or until well browned and firm to touch. If the pudding browns too quickly, cover it lightly with grease-proof paper and leave it to finish baking.

● Cool the pudding for about 15 minutes then brush with the apricot jam and scatter over the toasted shredded coconut.

● Serve with custard while still warm.

BAKED MANGOES AND BANANAS

SERVES 4

4 firm medium size ripe mangoes, sliced
2 ripe bananas, sliced   2 tsp brown sugar
juice of one lime   ½ tsp mixed spice
½ tsp vanilla essence
60 ml (2 fl oz) light brown rum
50g (2 oz) sweet desiccated coconut

● Pre-heat the oven to 190C (375F) or gas mark 5.

● Arrange the mango and banana slices in shallow oven-proof dish. Mix together the rest of the ingredients, except the desiccated coconut and pour over the fruit. Bake in the middle of the oven for 15-20 minutes. Sprinkle with desiccated coconut and serve with vanilla ice cream.

COCONUT ICE

These delicious coconut squares are everyone's favourite.
Freshly grated coconut is not as difficult as you might think.
The coconut can be broken into pieces and the flesh removed
from the shell. Put the flesh into a food processor with a
chopping blade or put small pieces into food processor
with a little liquid to help the grinding process.

MAKES 12-16
450g (1 lb) granulated or caster sugar
225g (8 oz) freshly grated or desiccated coconut
125 ml (4 oz) sweetened condensed milk
½ tsp almond essence
25g (1 oz) margarine
pink edible food colouring

● Put the sugar and milk in heavy based saucepan on low heat
and stir until the sugar has dissolved. Increase the heat slightly
and cook slowly for about 10 minutes. Quickly stir in the
grated or desiccated coconut together with the almond essence.
Pour half the mixture into a shallow square dish and spread
with a spatula.

● Mix a few drops of food colouring into the remaining
coconut mixture, then pour the pink coconut mixture over the
white bottom layer. Spread out the top layer evenly with a
spatula.

● Chill in the fridge for 10 minutes or until set. Mark out
12-16 squares, leave to cool completely then cut out the squares.

CASSAVA PONE

Cassava flour (garee/gari) can be reconstituted and desiccated
coconut can be used to make this recipe more quickly.
Either way, it is delicious.

MAKES 10-12

2 medium size cassavas (or 185g (6 oz) cassava flour)
the flesh of 1 medium coconut (or 185g (6 oz) desiccated coconut)
50g (2 oz) butter or margarine
100g (4 oz) brown sugar or caster sugar
150 ml (5 fl oz) water or milk
1 tbsp flour
1 tsp vanilla or mixed essence
½ tsp mixed spice
½ tsp salt
¼ tsp ground black pepper

● Pre-heat the oven to 180 C (350F) or gas mark 5.

● Peel, wash and grate the cassavas. Grate the coconut and mix
all ingredients together in a bowl. The mixture should be soft.

● Spoon the mixture into a shallow, square, greased oven-proof
dish or pan, level off and bake in the oven for about 1½ hours.
When cool cut the pone into 3 inch squares.

AUNTIE'S COCONUT BREAD

MAKES 2 LOAVES
the flesh of 1 coconut, grated
1 egg beaten
450g (1 lb) self raising wholewheat flour
225g (8 oz) plain white flour   225g (8 oz) brown sugar
225g (8 oz) butter or margarine
150 ml (5 fl oz) milk
100g (4 oz) raisins   50g (2 oz) chopped cherries
1 tsp baking powder   1 tsp mixed spice
1 tbsp mixed essence

● Pre-heat oven to 180C (350F) or gas mark 4.

● Sift the white flour, baking powder and salt into a large bowl. Add the wholewheat flour, mixed spice and butter or margarine. Mix together until the butter is evenly distributed and the mixture looks like dry pastry mix. Add the sugar, grated coconut and cherries to the flour mixture.

● Mix the essence into the beaten egg and add it to the flour mixture. Slowly add the milk and combine everything together with wooden spoon until it becomes a soft dough which leaves the sides of the bowl clean.

● Divide the dough into two greased and floured 1 lb loaf tins. Bake in the oven for about 1 hour.

● Remove the tins from the oven and leave the bread in the tins to cool for about 20 minutes. Turn out the bread on a wire rack to cool completely. Slice and serve or wrap in grease-proof paper for storing.

COCONUT BUNS

MAKES 10-12 BUNS

185g (6 oz) brown sugar
225g (8 oz) strong flour
185g (6 oz) margarine
2 tsp baking powder
½ tsp vanilla essence
1 tsp mixed spice
2 eggs lightly beaten
125g (4 oz) desiccated or freshly grated coconut

● Cream the margarine and sugar in a bowl. Sift the flour, baking powder and mixed spice, then add them to the creamed margarine. Add the beaten eggs, vanilla essence and lastly add the grated coconut. Mix everything together to medium soft consistency.

● Pre-heat the oven to 180C (350F) or gas mark 4.

● Drop tablespoons of the mixture into greased bun tins or waxed fluted cake cups. Place them on a baking sheet and bake in the oven for 20-30 minutes.

● Remove from the oven and sprinkle with caster sugar ,if desired, before leaving them to cool. Store in an air tight container.

COCONUT AND RAISIN LOAF OR PLAIT

450g (1 lb) strong flour (white or wholemeal)
125 ml (5 fl oz) warm milk   *125 ml (5 fl oz) warm water*
100g (4 oz) raisins   *75g (3 oz) margarine*
75g (3 oz) desiccated coconut   *2 tsp dried yeast*
3 tsp sugar   *1 tsp salt*
1 tsp ground cinnamon or mixed spice

● Stir the dried yeast and sugar into the milk and water and leave for about 10 minutes or until the mixture froths.

● Sift the flour and salt into a bowl. Rub in the margarine, stir in the yeast mixture, coconut, raisins and cinnamon. Mix together with a wooden spoon to form a dough. Turn out the dough onto a floured surface and knead until the dough is no longer sticky. Cover the dough and leave it to rise to double the size.

● Meanwhile pre-heat the oven to 200C (400F) gas mark 6.

● Knock back the risen dough and allow it to rest for 5 minutes. Divide the dough into three and roll each piece into a sausage shape (about 14 inches long) and plait them together. Place the plait on a baking sheet and brush with milk. If a plain loaf is preferred, shape the dough accordingly, place in a 2 lb loaf tin, brush with milk, cover and leave to rise for about 20 minutes.

● Bake the loaf in the oven for 30-40 minutes or until golden brown. Cool on a wire rack.

● This tea bread is best eaten sliced with butter.

'CUT AND COME AGAIN' CAKE

The name of this cake speaks for itself. In our household it's usually completely finished before the day is out!

175g (6 oz) self raising wholewheat flour
100g (4 oz) vegetable margarine
100g (4 oz) soft brown sugar
3 eggs
60 ml (2 fl oz) Guinness or Stout
225g (8 oz) mixed fruits coarsely minced
100g (4 oz) chopped dates
6 glacé cherries chopped   1 tsp mixed spice
2 tsp mixed essence   ½ tsp grated nutmeg
1 tbsp dark rum   a pinch of salt

● Pre-heat the oven to 180C (350F) or gas mark 4.

● Grease an 8 inch round cake tin then line it with grease proof paper.

● Mix the margarine and all the dry ingredients together in a large bowl. Add the eggs, Guinness, mixed essence and rum. Fold in with a wooden spoon until well mixed. Spoon the mixture into the greased tin and level off the top.

● Bake on the middle shelf of the oven for about 1 hour. Check to see if the cake is cooked by inserting the blade of a sharp knife into the middle. The blade should come away clean. When cooked, remove the cake from the oven and leave it to stand for ten minutes before turning it out onto a wire rack to cool completely.

RICH ORANGE SPONGE CAKE

This yellow sponge cake, as we call it in the Caribbean, is very popular. No table is without it on special occasions or tea time.

225g (8 oz) softened butter
225g (8 oz) caster or soft brown sugar
225g (8oz) plain flour
4 eggs
1½ tsp baking powder
1 tsp vanilla essence
grated rind of 1 orange

● Cream the butter and sugar in a large bowl until light and creamy. Beat the eggs until they are frothy and fold them into the butter mixture.

● Sift the flour and baking powder into mixture. Add the vanilla essence and grated orange rind and beat together well.

● Pre-heat the oven to 180C (350F) or gas mark 4.

● Grease and flour an 8 inch round cake tin or 1 lb loaf tin, or line with grease-proof paper. Spoon in the cake mixture and level off the top. Bake in the middle of the oven for about 1 hour.

● When the cake is cooked turn off the oven and leave the cake in the oven for about 10-15 minutes to cool slowly. This will prevent the centre of the cake from collapsing.

CRUSTY BREAD ROLLS

MAKES ABOUT 12 ROLLS
450g (1 lb) strong white flour
300 ml (10 fl oz) warm milk
50 g (2 oz) butter
1½ tsp dried yeast
1 tsp sugar
1 tsp salt

● Sprinkle the dried yeast into the lukewarm milk. Add the sugar, stir and leave in a warm place to rise (until the liquid becomes frothy).

● Meanwhile, sift the flour and salt into a bowl, then rub in the butter. Stir in the yeast mixture to make a soft dough.

● Turn out the dough onto a floured surface and knead it thoroughly until it is smooth and firm. Put the dough in a large greased bowl. Cover it with a clean towel and leave it to rise in a warm place until it is double the size (about 50 minutes).

● Pre-heat the oven to 230C (450F) or gas mark 8

● Knead the risen dough lightly for 2 or 3 minutes, then cut it into 12 pieces and shape them into rolls. Place the rolls well apart on a greased baking tray and brush with milk.

● Bake in the oven until golden brown (about 10-15 minutes). Cool on a wire rack.

COTTAGE LOAF

This recipe is for one large loaf.

15g (2 oz) fresh yeast or 1½ tsp dried yeast
300 ml (10 fl oz) warm milk
450g (1 lb) strong wholemeal flour or strong white flour
60g (2 oz) butter or margarine
1 egg beaten to glaze
1 tsp salt
1 tsp sugar

● Dissolve the fresh yeast in half the quantity of milk. If you are using dried yeast, sprinkle it into the milk and leave in a warm place for 10-15 minutes until the liquid froths.

● Put the flour, salt and sugar in a large bowl. Add the butter and rub it in well until it is like a fine crumble. Make a well in the pastry mixture and pour in the yeast liquid and any remaining milk. Mix with a wooden spoon to a soft but firm dough.

● Turn the dough onto a floured surface and knead it well until it is smooth and elastic. Place the dough in a clean, oiled bowl and cover with grease-proof paper and a clean tea towel. Leave it in a warm place for about 1 hour until double in size.

● Turn the dough onto a floured surface and knead it lightly. Cut off one-third of the dough and shape it into a round. Shape the remaining dough into a larger round and place the smaller round on top of the larger round. Push a lightly floured wooden spoon handle into the centre of the top of loaf to make an indentation. Cover and leave the loaf dough in a warm place for about 20-30 minutes until it doubles in size.

● Meanwhile, pre-heat the oven to 200C (400F) or gas mark 6.

● When loaf dough is sufficiently risen, brush it with beaten egg to glaze and bake it in the oven for 20-25 minutes until it sounds hollow when tapped at the bottom. Leave the loaf to cool on a wire rack.

'BAKES' OR FRIED DUMPLINGS

MAKES 10-12 BAKES
225g (8 oz) flour
200 ml (6 oz) milk
125 ml (4 fl oz) water
2 tsp baking powder
1 tbsp butter
½ tsp salt
vegetable cooking oil for shallow frying

● Sift the flour and baking powder in a bowl. Rub in the butter, sugar and salt, combine with milk and water to form a dough, then knead to a smooth texture. Break the dough into 10-12 pieces and roll them into balls, flatten the balls into circles about half an inch thick and 4-5 inches in diameter. Heat the oil in a frying pan and fry the bakes until they are golden brown in colour. Drain them on kitchen paper.

SAVOURY BREAD PLAIT

This savoury bread looks stunning on a buffet table
when sliced to show its colourful filling.

350g (12 oz) strong plain flour
140 ml (3 fl oz) warm milk
140 ml (3 fl oz) warm water
50g (2 oz) softened butter or margarine
1 egg, beaten
1 egg mixed with 1 tbsp water to glaze
1 tsp caster sugar
1 tsp salt
2 level tsp dried yeast

FOR THE FILLING
1 medium onion, finely chopped
2 cloves garlic, chopped and crushed or pressed
225g (8 oz) canned pimentos, finely chopped
1 yellow pepper, roasted and finely chopped
2 spring onions, finely diced
1½ tsp vegetable bouillon or seasoned salt

MAKING THE DOUGH

● In a small bowl, mix the warm milk and warm water together
with the sugar and yeast. Set it aside in a warm place for about
15 minutes until frothy.

● Sift the flour and salt into a large bowl and rub in the butter
or margarine. Add the yeast mixture and egg to the flour and

mix everything together to a dough which leaves the sides of the bowl clean. Turn the dough out onto a floured surface and knead it for about 10 minutes until smooth. Place the dough in a greased bowl, cover it with cling film and leave it to rise for about 30 minutes until it doubles in size.

TO MAKE THE FILLING

● Meanwhile, in a medium sized bowl, mix together the ingredients for the filling, except the egg and water for glazing, and leave to one side.

TO MAKE UP THE PLAIT

● Preheat the oven to 200C (400F) or gas mark 6.

● Re-knead the dough for 2 minutes, then divide it into three and roll each third into flat strips 12 inches long by 4 inches wide. Spoon the filling mixture down the centre of each strip of dough, bring the sides of the dough up to wrap around the filling and press the edges together to seal them. Roll the stuffed dough over so that the sealed edges are underneath.

● Place the three lengths of stuffed dough side by side and carefully plait them together until the whole length is plaited. Join the ends together neatly and tuck them under. Place the plait on a lightly greased baking tray and brush evenly with the egg and water wash. Cover with oiled cling film and set aside for ten minutes to allow it to rise again. Remove the cling film.

● Bake for 15 to 20 minutes at 200C (400F) or gas mark 6, then reduce the heat to 190C (375F) or gas mark 5, and bake for a further 15 to 20 minutes until the plait is golden brown. Remove the plait from the oven and leave it to cool on a wire rack.

PANCAKES

Pancakes are very popular due to their versatility.
They can be served traditionally with lemon and sugar or with
a variety of sweet or savoury fillings.
They look very appetising stacked or tiered

MAKES 8-10 PANCAKES
250 ml (10 fl oz) milk
100g (4 oz) plain flour or wholemeal flour
2 eggs
vegetable oil for frying
½ tsp salt

● Sift the flour and salt into a bowl. Break the eggs into the bowl and add the milk. Whisk everything together into a soft batter, adding a little water if the batter is not thin enough. Cover and set aside in the fridge for about 20 minutes. Whisk the pancake mixture again just before you are ready to fry the pancakes.

● Heat a dessertspoon of oil at a time in a frying pan. Add 3 tablespoons of batter to cover the bottom of the pan. Cook each side of the pancake.

● Continue cooking the batter as above until it is all used up.

MUNG BEAN PATTIES

450g (1 lb) short crust pastry
125g (4 oz) mung beans
1 medium onion finely chopped
1 egg beaten
2 cloves garlic finely chopped
½ red pepper
1 tbsp vegetable gee or 2 tbsp olive oil
1 tsp jerk seasoning
½ tsp corn flour
salt and pepper to taste

● Cook the mung beans until they are tender and almost mushy. Saute the onion and garlic in the vegetable gee or olive oil for about 3 minutes, then add the chopped red pepper, jerk seasoning and cornflour. Leave to simmer for 5 minutes. Season to taste and set aside to cool.

● Pre-heat the oven to 200C (400F) gas mark 6.

● Roll out the pastry lightly and thinly (1 cm/½ inch thick) and cut out rounds with a 10 cm (4 inch) pastry cutter. Place about a heaped dessertspoonful of bean mixture into the centre of each round. Wet the edges and fold the pastry over the filling, then press the edges together with your finger tips to seal them and form half-moon patties. Prick the top of each pattie many times and brush with beaten egg or milk.

● Place the patties on a greased and floured baking sheet and bake in the oven for about 30 minutes until they are golden brown.

PARATHA ROTI

MAKES 8-10 ROTI
450g (1 lb) strong white flour
250 ml (10 fl oz) water
1 tsp baking powder
1 tsp salt
1 tbsp condensed milk (optional)
2 tbsp vegetable gee, melted
vegetable cooking oil for basting
a griddle or heavy duty frying pan

● Sift the flour, salt and baking powder into a large bowl. Rub in the melted gee. Mix together the condensed milk and water, or just water, and add to the flour to make a dough. Knead the dough gently to a smooth texture. Cover the dough with a damp cloth or tea towel, allow it to rest for 10-15 minutes.

● Divide the dough into 8 to 10 pieces, kneading each piece until smooth. Roll out flat and thin each piece of dough, brush with oil and sprinkle lightly with flour. Roll up each flat piece of dough like a Swiss roll, cover with a moist towel and set aside for at least 1 hour.

● Heat the griddle or heavy duty frying pan.

● Flatten the dough rolls and roll out each piece again. Cook the roti one at a time as follows: brush with oil or gee place the roti on the hot griddle or frying pan. Turn the roti frequently brushing each side with oil to enable it to cook but not burn. Remove the roti and clap it with both hands until pliable and leafy in texture. Fold it in half and then in half again and arrange it on platter lined with grease-proof paper. Repeat the process until all the roti are cooked and arranged on the platter.

● Serve hot with vegetable curry.

FLOATS

Floats are light and fluffy split and filled
with the filling of your choice.

MAKES 8-10 FLOATS
225g (8 oz) plain flour
75g (3 oz) butter or margarine
150 ml (5 fl oz) warm water
1½ tsp dry yeast
½ tsp sugar
½ tsp salt
vegetable cooking oil for shallow frying

● Pour the warm water into a bowl, sprinkle in the sugar and yeast, stir to dissolve and leave in a warm place until the liquid becomes creamy.

● Meanwhile, mix the flour, salt and butter together like a crumble. Add the yeast liquid and enough water to make a soft dough. Knead well. Cover and leave in a warm place until the dough doubles in size.

● Cut the dough into 8 to 10 pieces, roll them into small balls. Cover and leave them to rise for about 10 minutes. Flatten the dough pieces to 4 inches in diameter. Heat the oil in frying pan and shallow fry until golden brown. Drain on kitchen paper.

DRINKS AND SYRUPS

These refreshing drinks and cocktails can look stunning.
They are an essential part of Caribbean meals and
entertainment. Served chilled or with ice
and colourful garnishes.

Fruit daiquiri
Mauby
Stout punch
Tropical fruit punch
Sorrel drink
Island cream punch
Coconut punch
Carambola punch
Carrot punch
Pawpaw milk shake
Fruitie smoothie
Ginger beer
Simple syrup
(Lemon and lime syrup)
Passion fruit syrup

FRUIT DAIQUIRI

This refreshing drink is even more delicious with rum added.

SERVES 2

2 limes juiced   50g (2 oz) sugar
125ml (4 fl oz) passion fruit juice
½ cup crushed pineapple   2 dashes of Angostura Bitters.

● Shake all the ingredients together then blend them with ice. Serve in cocktail glasses garnished with wedges of pineapple.

MAUBY

MAKES 2 LITRES

50g (2 oz) Mauby bark   1 cinnamon stick
2 litres water   225g (8 oz) sugar to taste
4 cloves   1 bay leaf

● Boil the Mauby bark, cinnamon stick, bay leaf and cloves in 700ml (25 fl oz) of water for 10-15 minutes. Let it cool and then add the remaining water and sugar. Leave to brew for a few minutes, then adjust for sweetness.

● Decant the drink into bottles and leave them in a cool place for a day or two. Serve with ice.

STOUT PUNCH

MAKES 1.5 LITRES

1 x 400g condensed milk   *1 tsp vanilla essence*
1 x 400g evaporated milk   *dash of Angostura bitters*
2 x 300 ml bottles of Stout   *100g (4 oz) brown sugar*
150 ml (5 fl oz) light brown rum (optional)
grated nutmeg

● Place all the ingredients, except the Stout and grated nutmeg, in a jug and mix well. Add the Stout, stir briskly and serve in tall glasses over ice garnished with grated nutmeg.

TROPICAL FRUIT PUNCH

Canned or fresh juices can be used in this punch.

MAKES 1.5 LITRES

300 ml (10 fl oz) orange juice   *300 ml (10 fl oz) grapefruit juice*
300 ml (10 fl oz) pineapple juice
50 ml (2 fl oz) lime or lemon juice   *225 ml (8 fl oz) ginger ale*
125 ml (4 fl oz) syrup   *dash Angostura Bitters*

● Mix all the ingredients in a large jug. Add the ginger ale just before serving. Serve chilled over ice.

SORREL DRINK

The sorrel used for this delicious drink is not the French kind used in salads or for cooking, but the red petals of the sorrel fruit which flowers at Christmas time in the Caribbean. No table is complete without Sorrel Drink or Sorrel Liqueur in the Caribbean!

MAKES 2 LITRES

2 litres (70 fl oz) boiling water
175g (6 oz) dried sorrel
1 stick of cinnamon
1 slice of dried orange peel
60 ml (2 fl oz) sweet sherry (optional)
sugar or honey to taste (about 6 to 8 oz)
dash of Angostura bitters
4-6 cloves
3 tbsp lime or lemon juice

● Put the sorrel petals into a large heatproof jug and pour on the slightly cooled, boiled water. Add the cinnamon stick and dried orange peel. Cover and leave to draw for 24 hours. Strain off the liquid, add the lemon or lime juice, angostura bitters, sherry (if liked) and sugar or honey to taste.

● Decant the sorrel drink into bottles, add one or two cloves to each bottle and store in the fridge. Serve well chilled or with ice in tall glasses.

ISLAND CREAM PUNCH

MAKES 1.5 LITRES

1 can of your favourite lager beer
3 eggs   juice of 1 lime
1 x 400g can sweet condensed milk
400 ml (15 fl oz) evaporated milk
250 ml (10 fl oz) light rum   ½ tsp grated nutmeg
1 tsp vanilla extract   3 tsp Angostura Bitters

● Whip the eggs together with the lime juice. Add the rum, both milks, the angostura bitters and blend well. Lastly, add the beer and pour into glasses with crushed ice.

COCONUT PUNCH

MAKES 1.5 LITRES

2 whole dry coconuts   1 litre (35 fl oz) warm water
1 x 400g can sweetened condensed milk
185g (6oz) sugar (optional)   1½ tsp almond essence
½ tsp grated nutmeg

● Make up coconut milk out of the two coconuts and the litre of warm water (see 'Essential Basics' page 22). Add the condensed milk, almond essence and grated nutmeg to the coconut milk and stir well. Chill the punch in the fridge and serve in tall glasses over ice.

CARAMBOLA PUNCH

SERVES 3
4-6 good sized carambola/star fruit
1 small carambola for garnishing
2 tbsp lemon or lime juice   sugar or honey to taste
¼ tsp nutmeg, grated   cracked ice

● Wash the fruit, cut it into large pieces and blend it in a blender until it is smooth. Strain the juice into a jug, add the lemon or lime juice and sweeten with sugar or honey to taste. Serve in tall glasses over cracked ice with a slice of carambola each and a sprinkling of grated nutmeg.

CARROT PUNCH

MAKES 1 LITRE
1 kilo (2 lb) carrots
200 ml (7 fl oz) sweetened condensed milk
300ml (11 fl oz) whole milk or soya milk
1 tsp vanilla essence   1 dash Angostura Bitters
pinch nutmeg

● Wash the carrots thoroughly and put them in a juice machine. Alternatively, chop them and liquidise them with water in a blender. Strain the carrot juice and add the remaining ingredients. Stir well and chill before serving.

Pawpaw (Papaya) Milk Shake

MAKES 2 GLASSES

1 medium sized pawpaw　　*250 ml (10 fl oz) milk*
75g (3 oz) caster sugar　　*pinch grated nutmeg for garnish*
1 cup crushed ice

● Peel the pawpaw and remove the seeds. Cut it into cubes. Blend it in a blender or pass it through a sieve. Add the sugar and milk and stir well. Add the crushed ice and blend until thick.

● Serve with grated nutmeg on top.

Fruity Smoothie

Great as a filling breakfast when time is short.
Any fruit is ideal but banana makes an excellent base.

SERVES 3

2 ripe bananas　　*12 strawberries*
1 large glass of your favourite fruit juice
125 ml (4 oz) plain yoghurt (optional)
pinch of grated nutmeg

● Blend ingredients together in a blender or liquidiser. Chill (if preferred) and serve.

GINGER BEER

Ginger beer, home made from fresh, green ginger is a
traditional Caribbean drink. This ginger beer
must be left to stand for 48 hours.

MAKES 2 LITRES
150g (6 oz) fresh green ginger
1 oz to 8 oz cane sugar according to taste
2 litres (70 fl oz) boiling water
half a lemon or lime
10 dried cloves

● Peel, wash and grate the ginger, put it in a large heat-proof
jug or jar and pour on the boiling water. Peel the lemon or lime,
add both the lime and the rind to the jug, then leave it at room
temperature for 48 hours.

● Strain the ginger beer and sweeten it to taste. Pour it into
clean bottles, add two or three dried cloves to each, cover and
leave to chill in the fridge or a cool place. Serve in tall glasses
over cracked ice.

PASSION FRUIT SYRUP

MAKES 2 LITRES

1 litre (35 fl oz) water   6 passion fruit pulped
500 ml (18 fl oz) passion fruit juice
1 kilo (2lb) sugar

● Mix the sugar and water together and heat until boiling. Add the passion fruit pulp. Boil for a further 20 minutes until the liquid begins to thicken. Remove from the heat and leave to cool. When cooled, strain and bottle.

SIMPLE SYRUP

MAKES 1 LITRE

1 kilo (2 lb) sugar
1 litre (35 fl oz) water

● Put all the ingredients in a saucepan and bring it to the boil. Simmer for 20 minutes until the syrup starts to thicken. Cool, strain and pour the syrup into bottles. Store in a cool place.

LEMON OR LIME SYRUP

This can be made by adding the juice of two lemons or two limes before the syrup cools.

INDEX

Index